THE
BULLETPROOF
HUSBAND

DR. JONATHAN WELTON

CO-AUTHORS ENDRE GABORI, JOHN SCANNELL, & DR. GARY MENEZES

TABLE OF CONTENTS

PART THREE

Either you trust, take ownership, and become bulletproof, or fail at life

ACKNOWLEDGMENTS

To the men of The Bulletproof Husband program, the men putting in the hard emotional work to make changes and step up for your wives and children, this book goes out to you – bravo!

To Endre Gabori, John Scannell and Dr. Gary Menezes. Thank you for the creating the program and materials that are building men, saving wives from emotional abuse and preventing children from going through the heartbreak of broken homes. Without you, I would have likely ended up as a divorced narcissist without any hope or future.

To my fellow coaches in the memberCoaches program, you are my brothers and heroes. It is an honor to know you and serve alongside you.

To my three daughters and my beautiful wife, you all gave me the motivation to fight my inner demons, to go to hell and back. I am eternally grateful for you.

PREFACE

My father left my mother in 1991 when I was 2 months shy of 5 years old. I was at daycare at the time, and out of everyone in our family, my father only chose to come and say goodbye to me. His decision was driven in part by his knowledge that I wouldn't understand the weight of his words. With me, he didn't have to deal with the repercussions of the responses his leaving would elicit from others who would have understood. Immediately after, he left and moved to Canada while we remained in Hungary.

My mother was devastated; I still remember consoling her at my bedside, letting her know, "don't worry, Mom. Everything will be ok." In 1996, I lost the last consistently present male figure in my life, my grandfather. At this point, I became very aware of the meaning of losing someone. It normalized for me, and I began to think that this must be part of life. My grandfather's passing also meant I would continue my childhood with my overprotective mother, my unstable sister (who also got crushed by my father's "exodus"), and my great-grandmother. This was a very heavy, feminine environment with zero masculine figures for me to follow. The consequences of this would be huge in all areas of my life.

School was challenging. Conversations with other boys became tough because their fathers taught them all sorts of cool stuff that I just couldn't relate to. I didn't have that knowledge. I didn't have that guidance. I felt like an outsider, and I was often made fun of for my lack of knowledge as well. Bullying was an everyday thing—being made fun of, called names, being picked on, and, sometimes, beaten up. As a result of this, I was not a great student. I always got by and did the minimum, but I was never the "first in class."

My sister's path also took a frantic turn, resulting in five abortions and four suicide attempts before the age of 23. One day, I had to watch the emergency responders rush into our house to "wash out" my sister's stomach in our bathtub after she swallowed a bottle of painkillers in her room. The whole tub was black, and my sister was on the floor barely breathing. She wouldn't have survived if the ambulance had arrived ten minutes later. My sister was constantly longing for my father's approval, for him to say, "I am proud of you."[1] All of these events further reinforced my mother's overprotective nature toward me, and I was even more coddled. (At least, she attempted to coddle me, but I always had a fire in my belly. It didn't work most of the time.)

My father would frequently send letters to my mother, but she would not respond. His visits were not so frequent. By 1993, I hadn't seen my father in 2 years. One afternoon, I was sat on my bed watching a cartoon when I looked to the side, and there he was. My father. It took a minute to register, but then I got up and ran to him. In '98 my mother and father decided for me that I should move to Canada. I have no idea to this day how my mother agreed to the move after all that had happened. What kind of sacrifice and lack of ego it must have taken for her to make that happen.

In 2006, after four years back in Hungary, I decided to return to Canada to start school at the University of Toronto. I still had that fire in my belly, and even though I didn't know what was driving me, I knew in my gut it was the right move to make. Staying in Hungary wasn't going to cut it, and even with my tense relationship with my father, the odds still looked better in Canada. This time, the move was my choice.

1| I am heartbroken to say that on February 6, 2023, my sister succeeded in taking her own life because of her unresolved issues. She saw no other way out.

To my surprise back then, the insecurities (bullets) and survival behaviors developed in my childhood also got on the plane with me. I couldn't find myself, and I didn't know what it meant to be authentic. I constantly tried to please everyone I met at university, afraid to be confronted and/or not approved of. Then came the 3 most significant turning points in my life to finding myself:

January 4, 2011, the month of October 2011, and the summer of 2015.

On January 4, 2011, I started my first "real" job in Toronto, having just turned 24 years old (this is also where I met my wife). It was a sales job for a software company. I was the underdog no matter how you looked at it. Youngest, least experienced, least professional looking, least respected, least sought out. I even had an accent. In many ways, everybody thought I was a joke. All the odds were stacked against me. Nonetheless, I was a driven overworker with no social life, who was also quite unhappy.

During my first month, I had an epiphany and a question popped in my head—what do I have on these guys that they don't? Then it hit me—a crazy personality with extreme persistence and a much higher-than-average risk tolerance (which are both still present to this day, but were, back then, clearly driven by my insecurities). I thought, what do I have to lose? I went all in...

I started researching. I started dialing. I started to be pushy (in a creative and funny way) with companies. I said stuff on the phone that to this day I have no clue how I got away with. I remember heads turning beside me when I was on the phone with companies. There were times when even management came over to listen in on my calls.

Lo and behold, the results started to show. That year, I became the #1 sales guy out of a dozen plus people with years of experience and President's Club awards behind them. I destroyed EVERYBODY in sales.

That same year, I got really close with a sales colleague, Quentin.

He showed me another way to live, and how my struggles may have more to do with me than others. He was a man I looked up to, and I valued his opinion. He was so masculine, so well put together, and so confident. He didn't care what anybody said to him; he had that kind of confidence in himself. His grounded confidence inspired me, and I found myself wanting to be like him. He also saw through me. It was very obvious to him that I had unresolved father challenges. As a result, one day when we were driving home (we used to carpool together) he said, "Are you interested in a better way to live your life?"

That one sentence took me on one of the most experiential personal development journeys in my life and made me unstoppable. Unstoppable with day-by-day growing confidence. I found a way to let go of blaming my father, with whom my relationship was growing daily. I started to understand why my mother and my sister act the way they act. I got rid of 90% of my friendships and built new meaningful ones. I married the best woman on this planet, who would become the mother of my daughters. It was an intense time of growth and introspection, and my life was finally on a high.

I left the company 2 years later, hopping from one place to another in an attempt to understand the evergrowing fire in my belly. I still didn't know where it would lead me, but I knew with skyrocketing confidence that I was on the right path and that my purpose was to make a difference on a mass scale. What I had learned was too valuable to keep a secret, and I had to find a way to clarify these lessons. In the summer of 2015, I left the corporate world and went out on my own doing sales contracting. At the same time, my mind was constantly thinking about how to make a difference in the world.

During this discovery, I volunteered in men's groups on a weekly basis. Again, I was the youngest, but my ability to help men was very clear to everybody. It didn't matter if it was marriage, confidence, or other life-related topics. Although, I excelled at marriage. Some of the men I helped had sons older than me, but despite their greater age, I was still able to get through to them. So from age 24 to 30 I was helping one man at a time.

Then in 2017, while taking a shower (where many of my ideas begin), it all came to me and got crystalized. I could merge my experience in sales and business with my desire to get these lessons out in the world. The result: The Bulletproof Husband.

I immediately called Gary Menezes (co-author of this book), who was my business/life coach since summer of 2015 (and also, in a way, a father figure). I knew Gary from my volunteering, where he was one of the senior leaders. I saw his vast experience in creating training for men. He was very successful in business, and I knew he could help me merge these worlds of business and training men, helping me bring my vision into reality.

In addition, I knew I needed to find the right business partner. This is where John Scannell, co-founder of The Bulletproof Husband, co-author of this book, and a friend for over a decade comes in. John represents everything The Bulletproof Husband stands for—he is solid, consistent, and reliable. I have always been drawn to John's clarity of thought—his ability to see a bigger picture outside of whatever challenge or decision was currently on the table.

My path crossed with John's at a time early in my immersed self-development journey. Here was a man who had literally lost millions in the property crash of 2008/2009. Here was a man who was recently divorced, and although he did not have children at the time, he was committed to figuring out why his life had been turned upside down and how he had contributed to that. Like me, John had emigrated to Canada; he is one of the tallest leprechauns to leave the island of Ireland. Unlike me, John's childhood was very different. John is an only son to parents who will celebrate their 55th wedding anniversary this year. John grew up with 5 sisters, one of whom is his twin sister. He often jokes that he didn't even get 9 months on his own without having a female figure in his life.

Despite this powerful female presence in his life, John was a solid man when we met, a man who didn't need to lead from the front but could do so by just being him. To this day, he is still that man. He is competitive in what matters to him, which is to be better today than he was yesterday. He is egoless in his interactions with others because that is not who he is competing against.

Why are John and I business partners? Because we are so much more than that. We are mission partners. We are both aligned in making a difference in children's lives by making a difference with men. We hold each other responsible and to account for our mission. The similarities of our skill sets allow us to be excited about our mission. The diversity of our skill sets allows us to execute on our mission.

John did figure out the "why." Clear on his responsibility and ownership, he is happily married to a woman who continues to inspire him to be more, to be better; not only for her, but also for their three young children. John is not only a Bulletproof Husband, he is also a Bulletproof Father. I have witnessed him navigate the journey of his child being diagnosed with leukemia and undergoing years of treatment. While I hope that is never a path I need to walk in relation to my daughters, looking at him gives me clarity about what it looks like to be a solid, consistent, and reliable leader of my family if I do.

Endre Gabori
Co-Founder of *The Bulletproof Husband*

PURPOSE

"Empower husbands to be the best version of themselves so that no child has to experience the pain of a broken home."

The psychology of how a marriage breaks down follows a very specific pattern in almost all cases. In that pattern, the husband only chooses to seriously work on their marriage when in the eyes of the wife "it is too late." This becomes the average husband's starting point when engaging The Bulletproof Husband.

To be able to help husbands rebuild their families after they have gotten, what we call, the "slap" is very fulfilling for all parties involved. The degree of transformation that husbands experience after implementing the work of The Bulletproof Husband (regardless if their marriage is saved or not) is quite extraordinary.

The fact is that men of today are often very quick to jump to conclusions and make irrational decisions in their marriage that cause significant damage to their family, which they only realize later. Most of these originate in unresolved insecurities and biases that have developed over their lifetime due to hurts and vulnerabilities which they have not faced and dealt with.

Yes, both parties (wife and husband) have responsibilities in why the marriage is not working. In The Bulletproof Husband, we chose to focus on the masculine, bringing a deep understanding to the differences between the feminine and masculine, and giving husbands the tools necessary to lead their families and bring the best out of their wife (including her healthy feminine side). We made a decision to empower these husbands with tools and structures that will not only serve them, but the thousands of lives they will each touch as a result of their work.

Here at The Bulletproof Husband, we are convinced that being a good father and husband is your obligation regardless of your feelings. Remember, your child didn't ask to be born. You and mom made that decision for them. This came with a commitment (whether you knew it or not) that is greater than your ego and your feelings. Your actions today can have ripple effects for your children decades down the road. It is vital to never, ever forget that.

In addition, we are on the mission of ensuring that within the next 15-20 years The Bulletproof Husband's work will be taught in the public education system across North America to help promote healthy masculinity, as well as to help young male adults get set up for success in life and relationships.

ENDORSEMENT OF DR. JONATHAN WELTON

When I first met Doctor Jonathan Welton, in my capacity as a leader in The Bulletproof Husband, he was facing marital challenges, co-parenting challenges, and was also kicked out of his highly sought after position in ministry. Just like any of our raving fans or endorsers,[2] he started his journey with us as a member of The Bulletproof Husband.

When Doc Jon (as we call him) joined The Bulletproof Husband, he was at the lowest point in his life. Desperate, just like any other husband who has tried to resolve their marital challenges unsuccessfully by themselves, he too decided to reach out for help.

Upon joining The Bulletproof Husband, it was immediately clear that Doc Jon had several "big walls of protection" set up in his life, which didn't allow him to see the "root causes" of his behaviors and the damage it brought with it. With the help of The Bulletproof Husband and Doc Jon's dedicated and consistent implementation of the tools, structures, and systems, he quickly got to the bottom of it all in record time.

2| (www.bulletproofhusband.com/wall)

Once he did this, the results started to come one after the other. He was able to reconcile with his wife Karen and build a brand-new relationship with the same woman with whom there was no light at the end of the tunnel just a few months prior. The relationship with his children took on new heights of leadership and fathering. Doc Jon's ability to spread his knowledge and experience started to be felt by all members of The Bulletproof Husband.

But this wasn't enough for him. He wanted to raise his game even more with his new-found confidence and desire to make a difference on a massive scale.

Doc Jon embarked on a rigorous 1-year certification training by memberCoaches Inc. (which we started to expand The Bulletproof Husband's reach) to allow him the ability to coach members in an official capacity. He successfully completed that and, during this training, he also got reinvited back to the ministry. As of me writing this, Doc Jon also holds the record for the "most husbands referred to The Bulletproof Husband" (by far).

If all stars hadn't already aligned at this point, they definitely did when The Bulletproof Husband leaders, who had been contemplating writing a book like this for some time, were approached by Doc Jon with the desire to do just that for us. Yes, we decided that somebody who has written 12 books already (2 of which are bestsellers) probably would be more equipped to articulate the concepts of The Bulletproof Husband than myself or any other member of leadership. Another upside to it is that there is no better way to let people know about The Bulletproof Husband than by having a successful member write it himself.

Doc Jon was perfect, as an experienced author and model of our success, but we did have a little concern about such a devout man. The Bulletproof Husband is a "religion-neutral" organization, which means that we welcome husbands from all walks of life, regardless of their religious background. It also means that the tools taught do not cater to or derive from any religious source, being instead purely based on various psychological foundations. Not surprising, he was willing to keep our "religious-neutral" view toward the book, and he dove in, putting pen to paper. Here we are today.

With all of that said, a special thank you needs to be said to Doc Jon for his dedication, tenacity, persistence, and his unbelievable ability to be a team player without ego. Words cannot describe The Bulletproof Husband leadership's gratitude for helping us spread the word, the knowledge, and for bringing us closer to a future vision that will change generations to come.

Thank you.

Be the bowl,

Endre Gabori
Co-Founder of *The Bulletproof Husband*

INTRODUCTION

I remember standing in my kitchen, tears streaming down my face, as I realized the impact that this would have on my three young daughters. My wife had just told me to get out, that we were separating, that we were likely getting divorced. It was April 2020, and Covid-19 lockdowns were in full swing.

Up to this point, I had spent my adult life in full-time ministry. I had received a Doctorate Degree in Ministry, written a dozen books including two best-sellers, and traveled to 35 countries lecturing and leading archeological tours. A few years earlier, I had started an online Bible school and had 2,600 students enrolled from all over the world.

I was intelligent, charming and highly respected far and wide, yet behind closed doors, I was a total asshole. I didn't know it at the time, but I had zero self-awareness of how I was treating the people around me. It wasn't only my wife that was sick of my shit, it was also my employees, my pastor and my close friends; the list was long. They tried so hard to help me see how I was behaving, but to no avail. I would constantly argue, lie, manipulate, defend, deflect, minimize, blame-shift, and I would never take any responsibility for my actions. I took advantage of the trust and respect that people had for me to self-medicate my emotional wounds. This included having emotional affairs as well as loads of inappropriate communication and behavior with staff members.

Finally, everyone had had enough. In my stubborn hard-headedness, I drove my life to rock bottom. I got myself excommunicated from my church, I lost countless friends, my employees wrote blogs about how I had treated them, and my board put out a letter warning everyone to stay away from me because I was a toxic leader. After all this, my wife had been standing with me, but eventually she reached her limit. The final straw for her was that I still didn't see how I had hurt all these people and made them feel – my total lack of empathy was a huge red flag. Another red flag was my continued inability to take any ownership of my behaviors or to change them.

So I moved out the next morning. This was my second time of being separated in the last three years, and I was at absolute rock bottom.

As I lay on a children's canopy bed at my parents' house, I tried to figure out how to repair the massive mess I had made of my life. I had been watching these free videos from this online program called The Bulletproof Husband (TBH). I didn't really know what I was signing up for, but they seemed really confident about their ability to help men in my situation. I finally just signed up.

Now, looking back, I can say that joining The Bulletproof Husband was one of the best decisions of my adult life. At the time that my wife kicked me out, her psychologist had told her, "Your husband is a narcissist and in 40 years of clinical practice I have not seen men like your husband change." But 90 days later, he was calling my transformation "a miracle" and said, "Whatever they are doing in his group, it is working. He has made all the changes I didn't expect him to make!" Around that time, my wife invited me home and our marriage has been on an upward trajectory ever since.

Although this book isn't about my story, I will sprinkle it throughout in the hopes that it inspires you to read on. After relentlessly trying so many methodologies, I can tell you without a shadow of a doubt that the tools I am going to show you in this book can dramatically alter you as a man and change your marriage, your family and all the relationships in your life.

Here's my disclaimer: I didn't create the tools you are about to receive in this book. I am a student of TBH and as the first certified coach in their training program, I have been entrusted with writing this book and using my voice to share these tools with the world. I consider it a great honor and a weighty responsibility to share with you what saved my marriage and made me into the man I always wanted to be.

Dr. Jonathan Welton
December 2022

THE RELATIONSHIP ROADMAP

1
THE SLAP!

Getting "the slap" means getting a wakeup call. It could be the heart attack that leads you to losing weight and finally getting healthy. Or it could be the vacation denial from your boss that finally pushes you to quit your job to launch that entrepreneurial venture you have been procrastinating about. When the slap hits a marriage, it can be finding out she is cheating, or her telling you she wants a separation and you need to get out, or it could be the courier handing you divorce papers you had no idea were coming. The shock, pain and the broken heart that each man feels when he gets the slap is deep and terrifying.

I received multiple slaps before I woke up. Slap #1 was September 18, 2018. That's when my advisory board sent an email to my online students informing them that the school was closing immediately and indefinitely, and that I was not fit to lead. This was quickly followed by slap #2 where my wife kicked me out. My wife was eight months pregnant at the time with our third child. I imploded our entire world, our reputation, our finances, our relationships, and all about five weeks before my wife would go into labor. She didn't even know if she wanted to have me at the birth at the time. Our marriage was hanging by a thread.

I got to work on myself as hard and fast as possible. I hired a counselor to work with for an hour a day for the next three months. I made some progress and thankfully my wife allowed me to attend the birth of our child. After the birth, the separation continued until around New Year's, when she invited me back home.

We then had a little over a year of peace where we thought our marriage was doing great. One of my board members even wrote three chapters about our healing process in a book he published during that year. Unfortunately, we didn't realize then how much deeper we still needed to go. The picture that comes to mind would be of a 450lb man losing 50lbs and thinking he feels worlds better and is doing so much better. Yes, he has made progress, yet to be accurate, he has a long way to go. By March of 2020, slap #3 happened. My board sent out a letter telling the public that I still wasn't doing better and I had a long way to go. Then slap #4 happened when my pastor (who had also been my best friend in previous years) sent me an official letter excommunicating me from the church. Slap #5 was when some of my former staff published blogs sharing how I abused their trust and acted inappropriately, especially as a married minister with another child on the way. Slap #6 was in late April 2020 when my wife kicked me out a second time. She had finally reached her breaking point and this furious round of slaps 3–6 were the ones to shift me from wanting to change, to knowing that I HAD TO change.

Once the slap occurs there are a few typical responses from most men: clinging, pleading, begging, looking for tools and resources, finally reaching out for a marriage counselor, arguing, blaming, or feeling like a victim. When a man gets the slap, he falls into an emotional pit and doesn't know his ass from his elbow. For me, I had tried everything I could get my hands on after the first two slaps. So when I got slaps 3–6, I signed up for The Bulletproof Husband as a last-ditch effort.

Looking back, I now thank God for each and every one of my slaps, they have made me into the man I am today. See, getting the slap from a wife is the wakeup call that most men need at some point in their marriage journey. Typically, a wife has been evaluating and contemplating giving the slap for about two years before she gives it. During that time, she is testing her man, poking at his insecurities, trying to goad him into action. Yet men typically don't make the needed changes until they get the slap, until change becomes a MUST.

The reason the slap wakes a man up is because *to a man, love feels like acceptance.* So when a woman sends the message "You are no longer acceptable to me the way that you are," it rocks a man's world. It shakes him the way a heart attack wakes up the man who needs to lose 200lbs.

The slap is the beginning of a journey. A journey that breaks all men — some are broken for the better and others are broken for the worse. This book will give you the tools and guidance needed for your post-slap journey.

My promise to you is this: if you do the emotional work and apply these tools, you will eventually be overwhelmingly grateful for the slap and for the man that it helped you become.

Here's a vision to keep in front of yourself: Picture you and your woman at 80 years old sitting on the porch of your house in rocking chairs. As you look over the yard, your grown children cooking at the BBQ and your grandchildren are playing in the grass. Your wife turns to you with affection and says, "Thank you for doing the hard emotional work to become the man I always knew you could be; I am so proud to be your wife." You respond, "Thank you for giving me the wake-up slap I needed to finally change." If you don't implement the tools in this book, you likely won't get there, but if you apply this book in your life, you have a shot! If you just learn the concepts in this book but you don't implement them in your life, you simply get the booby prize, not the real gold.

WARNING: I have seen countless men tell their story of slaps as a tale of woe and victimhood. If you don't do the emotional work of Stage Zero, you will stay in the pain of blame and irresponsibility, which guarantees the death of your relationship.

A HELPFUL CONTEXT: THE BUCKET OF PAIN

My wife said something I have heard thousands of other wives say because of The Bulletproof Husband. "Why does it take a slap for a man to finally deal with himself?! Why can't he just listen to her over the years and actually wake up and take care of his issues?" When she asked me, I remember the answer just flowing out of my mouth as a picture: it's as if each man is carrying around a bucket of brutal emotional pain. He is terrified to look into that bucket or deal with it. It is his greatest challenge and he will avoid it all costs. If he doesn't deal with that pain, he will live in reaction to that bucket. It's not until his wife draws a line in the sand and says, "Either you deal with that bucket of pain, or I am going to leave you, take your children, you will lose your money and your reputation" – that's when he will *consider* dealing with the bucketful of stuffed down emotional pain. The world of pain she is about to inflict must outweigh the pain of looking into that bucket and finally dealing with it. That is the leverage required for most men to change.

2
STAGE ZERO: GRIEVING THE SLAP

After my final slap, I was devastated. I was in such a world of hurt and hopelessness. Thankfully TBH laid out a clear path forward. I would have easily ended up like most men: stuck in the pit of the slap for years to come. Simply feeling like a victim and blaming others for slapping me. Yet TBH gave me the roadmap of Stage Zero to Stage Five, and so I got to work on Stage Zero.

If you've gotten the slap, then you've been slapped into Stage Zero. So welcome to hell! Stage Zero is the hurt, anger and feelings of loss that come from having received the slap. You knew there were some problems, but you didn't know she was cheating on you, or you didn't think she was about to leave you, kick you out or have divorce papers served. Now you are feeling yourself falling into a deep well of emotions. "Should I go to a therapist?" "Should I get on some medication?" "Should I fight back?" "Should I retaliate and tell her family what she is doing?" "Should I demand to stay in the house?" "Should I lawyer up?" "Should I beg and plead for her to stay?" "Should I guilt her about how it will affect the children?" "Should I try to win her back with love notes and flowers?" These and a hundred more thoughts could be racing through your mind. Every person you turn to will be giving you different advice, and you need to be aware that their advice is likely to be in *your* best interest, not in the relationship's best interest. It is a rare gem to have a friend who will challenge you to grow into the kind of man you need to be to fix your relationship.

So what do you really need to do in Stage Zero? What is the only way forward? How do you get out of the pit of despair, emotion, depression, anger, blaming and judgment?

You must proactively pull the anger and hurt out of yourself. Anger is the bodyguard that is blocking you from feeling the deep hurt and sorrow that is underneath. So start with anger.

Go somewhere private (e.g. the woods, an empty house, a car in an empty parking lot), and begin to rage. Scream, cry, curse, say whatever you need to say, call her every name in the book, keep nothing bottled up, get it all out, every last stinking drop of anger. Stay with the feeling until you feel it pass – there may be another wave, so let that out too. Once all the anger has passed, wait – often after a few moments of the anger being out, the hurt will come to the surface: crying, wailing, bawling your eyes out, shrieking, uncontrollable pain will come through you. Don't rush this process or avoid it. This is deep work and it is your priority right now.[1]

Once you have done this process, you will feel lighter and clearer,

---

1| Masssive Warning: I will repeat this whenever we are talking about letting out your emotions and pulling out your bullets. You must have high confidence before you start, otherwise the emotional work will actually drag you down into the depths of self-pity and self-blame. Pulling bullets while having low confidence can actually be dangerous for you mentally, emotionally and physically. After you complete doing emotional work, build your confidence back up again then move on with your day. The tools for managing your confidence can be found in the chapter entitled, "Got That Big D*ck Energy." Doing emotional work is one of the hardest things you will ever do and also one of the most important. For this reason alone, I would urge any man to join the Bulletproof Husband online program by going to www.BulletproofHusband.com/DocJon

and you will be one step closer to moving into Stage One. It often takes multiple sessions of this proactive emotional work to get the pain of the slap out of the way. Stage Zero can ideally be dealt with within two weeks of the slap, as long as you are doing this deep emotional work as often as needed, perhaps even twice a day or more.

WARNING: During Stage Zero, it is best to avoid conversing with your partner. Until you have dealt with your emotions from the slap, you are likely to cause more harm than good. If you must communicate, keep it clear, direct and to the point for now. Focus on the emotional work; there will be time to communicate later.

If you don't proactively do the emotional work to get the anger out, you can live in Stage Zero for years. If you don't get through Stage Zero, you will likely end up divorced unless she is fool enough to take you back.

3
THERE'S A GUN TO YOUR CHILD'S HEAD

To walk from Stage Zero to Stage Five requires a mountain of work from a man. Why should you do all this work?

By having your marriage fail, you are allowing life to put a gun to the head of your child. You have the power to change much of this, but let's look at the raw data of how divorce affects children.

EMOTIONAL DAMAGE TO CHILDREN OF DIVORCE

- Lower grades in school and are less pleasant to be around, based on a study of feedback from their peers
- 3x higher probability of the need for psychological help year over year
- 2–3x higher probability of committing suicide
- Higher probability of having a lower paying career
- Unstable father-child relationship, which has a different impact for daughters and sons

- Higher probability of drug and alcohol abuse
- Fears about commitment and divorce

PHYSICAL DAMAGE

- Higher cases of injury, asthma, headaches and speech defects
- 50% probability of having health problems
- Most molested children come from single-parent households
- A child in a female-headed home is 10x more likely to be physically assaulted or murdered

LONG-TERM EFFECTS

- Children from divorced parents are more likely to be lonely, unhappy, anxious, and insecure
- 70% of long-term prison inmates grew up in a broken home
- 2x higher probability of dropping out of high school
- Lower self-esteem, trust issues, less friendly

No woman wants these outcomes for the children they carried for nine months, gave birth to, nursed day and night, for whom they changed diapers and fretted over endlessly. Mothers naturally want the best for their children.

Yet, women are also the ones that initiate 80% of divorces!

How can this be?

This comes from one of the core differences between the masculine and the feminine. *The masculine acts and then feels, whereas the feminine feels and then acts.*

For a mother to expose her own children to the extreme danger of divorce, she must feel that she is saving those children from a greater danger of remaining married to an absolute asshole.

The only thing that can actually change that outcome is if the husband does the deep transformative work of changing permanently so that a woman's feelings can change back to feeling safe and avoid putting her children through the trauma of divorce.

Your children are going to be hurt by your bad marriage and statistically, they are likely to be significantly more damaged by a divorce, so really the only remaining option is that the same man who led the marriage to crash into the ditch at the side of the road now steps up and leads the marriage back to emotional safety once again.

When a man will do that, a woman's feelings can change and her actions will follow.

Obviously, most men pick up this book hoping to save their marriage, and yet your wife is going to say discouraging things along the way. She will say things like, "I don't care that you are working on yourself," "It's too little, too late," "I'll never have feelings for you again," "I have moved on," etc. The truth, though, is that if you have kids together, at a minimum you will be co-parenting them until they are 18 years old.

The work of Stage Zero up to the end of Stage Two needs to be done just to clean up the mess of you being a crappy husband, so you can have a productive co-parenting relationship. Then the work of Stage Three and Four can be done so that you can build a new romantic relationship and your children can grow up in an emotionally secure, committed environment.[2] Remember this: your children didn't ask to be born; that was a choice you and your wife made, so your children are your responsibility and you are obligated to do right by them.

Here is my advice to you. *Don't focus on trying to win your wife back.* Any strategy based primarily on that goal will really just be short-term manipulation. Focus instead on three goals:

2| Suffice it to say, there are endless studies and statistics on the Internet that show the emotional damage caused by parents divorcing, especially in the areas of suicidal ideation, depression, physical health, school dropout rates, etc.

1. Become the man you have always wanted to be.
2. Become the man you want your sons to be like when they grow up.
3. Become the kind of man you want your daughters to marry.

Those three focuses are a far healthier motivation to aim toward. If you work toward those three things, then you will become the kind of man your wife would be a fool to leave.

Lastly, at the end of the day, you may say to yourself, "Why give someone love and trust ever again? I'm only going to get hurt." Well, yes, love and trust will absolutely hurt you and shred your heart at times, but it's worth it. As Lord Alfred Tennyson wrote, *"Tis better to have loved and lost than never to have loved at all."* The goal isn't to avoid hurt, but to learn how to process your feelings responsibly and move forward rather than suppress them.

4
STAGE ONE: CREATING SPACE

"If you knew your potential to feel good, you would ask no one to be different so that you can feel good. You would free yourself of all of that cumbersome impossibility of needing to control the world, or control your mate, or control your child. You are the only one who creates your reality. For no one else can think for you, no one else can do it. It is only you, every bit of it you."

– Esther Hicks

The best $75 I ever spent was buying a used punching bag. After a couple of weeks of Stage Zero and letting out the anger, hurt and blame, I was ready to jump into Stage One. At first, Stage Zero felt so foreign. I was used to shoving my feelings down and being a nice guy on the surface. I was not in touch with how many suppressed feelings I had bottled up. Once I began to follow the program, I would put in my earbuds, blast some heavy metal music and punch and scream as loud as I could in my garage for about 20 minutes nonstop. At a certain point, I would pause when it felt like I was at the end of the anger and I would hug the punching bag because of exhaustion, and then the tears and wailing would flow out. In those moments, I deeply felt the fear of how divorce would affect my children and how I had failed them as a father. I would picture the pain in my wife's eyes that I had caused, or how I had let down everyone that had ever believed in me, and so on. By the time I was done, I was a limp noodle and there was a circle of sweat and tears all over the garage floor. Then the work of Stage One began.

STAGE ONE

If you have made it out of Stage Zero and arrived at Stage One, it's time to celebrate! You have already done a truckload of emotional work to reach this point. Take a moment to yell something in celebration. Really let yourself feel it, raise an invisible glass in the air and toast yourself on your success so far. I know it sounds silly, but get over your awkward self, get out of your head and actually reward yourself with a moment of celebration.

As you move forward into Stage One, always keep an eye out for more layers of anger. If you find them, use the tools from Stage Zero: find a place to be alone and responsibly dig out the anger and hurt until it is all gone.

The goal of Stage One is *having her feel safe, respected and as free as if she were already divorced.* This takes away the need for her to push for an immediate divorce. After divorce, she won't need your permission or approval for what she does, buys, or who she spends time with.

It is in this stage that she may be talking about "finding herself again," and your best plan of action is to give her the space to be her own person.

In Stage One, you don't have the right to loyalty, respect,

communication or anything else from her. Your feelings are not going to be her priority. Instead, you must let go of all your expectations. The old relationship and everything you used to know is dead and gone – and that's okay! You are aiming at building something new, and the old house must be razed first.

The objective of Stage One is to *make delaying the divorce more appealing than pursing it, and to restore her sense of safety and freedom.*

At this stage, you should only be focused on working on yourself, so you can become capable of working on the marriage later. While you are in Stage One, your presence is still pushing your wife toward divorce. This may not be intentional, but the momentum of your previous years of behavior is still rolling. This means that you want to deal with Stage One as soon as possible and revisit the principles here whenever she feels emotionally unsafe or controlled by you.

I remember my wife inviting me over to the house during Stage One simply to do housework for her. One afternoon, while working on some house project, she came to me and said, "I think we may have to sell the house because of our finances falling apart, and I may have to go live on my mom's couch." I responded simply: "I understand and will support you in whatever you need." Then she came back 10 minutes later to say, "Do you think our friends in North Carolina will be disappointed that we aren't moving down there?" "Yes, of course they will be disappointed." "Oh, okay…" Then she came back another 10 minutes later to say, "I think we should plant a row of arborvitae bushes in the back yard." "Yeah, sure babe, show me where you want them." And the next day I was at Home Depot renting a hole-digging auger and planting 26 bushes in the back yard. This whole story still makes me laugh; it is such a clear example of the splashing of the feminine. Basically the content of what she had to say wasn't important: in Stage One it is about giving her the feeling of freedom and removing all control and arguing from the relationship.

STRATEGIES FOR STAGE ONE

1. REMOVE ALL JUDGMENTS AND EXPECTATIONS YOU HAVE OF HER.

You have years of expectations built up from your old relationship. She has built up layers of resentment and regret from living under your expectations and that is a burden that you must remove from her shoulders. Start to interact with her as a new woman, as someone you don't know. Take nothing for granted; she owes you nothing.

2. NEXT BE ON THE LOOKOUT FOR YOUR CONTROLLING BEHAVIOR.

Any controlling behavior is going to push her toward divorce faster. Control shows up in a lot of forms. It can be demanding, shaming, or acting helpless and needy. All of these put emotional pressure on her to do something that she doesn't want to do and they all need to stop. It's not about your intentions – your intentions don't matter. What matters is making her feel emotionally safe and free, and not like you are pushing and pressuring her for something.

3. STOP BEING EMOTIONAL AROUND HER.

Remove your anger, frustration, irritation, hurt, sadness, neediness or clinginess. If you feel these emotions bubbling up within you, use an *exit strategy,* like "I have to make a phone call," "I have to go to the toilet," "I forgot I had to take care of something at the office," and just leave. Get out of there. Then, once you are alone, get the emotion out. Cry, scream, yell, weep, gut yourself until the tank is empty.

4. CHECK FOR YOUR BULLET WOUNDS.

If you find that you can't stop being controlling or having expectations, then you have found one of your *bullet wounds.* A bullet is a pocket of suppressed emotional pain, usually from childhood. Start with the pain you are currently feeling in the present, feel it fully and express it out of yourself. Once that has passed, intentionally search your heart for other times you felt the same way in the past. Let those feelings out too. Keep digging and letting out any other feelings. For example, she says she is leaving you, so you feel the pain and fear of abandonment. Once you let that out, you look in your heart and recognize that same fear of abandonment from when you broke up with several previous girlfriends; let that out too. Then you might recognize the same fear of abandonment from when your dad died when you were very young; grieve that moment too. Keep going until you have expressed all the feelings that you have been pushing down. Doing emotional work like this is the hardest work a man can do. Most men will not truly do this emotional work and will instead carry around their suppressed hurt for their whole life, while they get divorced and remarried over and over, sever the relationships with their children and friends, get repeatedly fired or crash their businesses. It doesn't matter if you are Bill Gates, Jeff Bezos, Elon Musk or one of most of the handsome men in Hollywood – a man's suppressed hurt will bring divorce to his doorstep.

5. TAKE RESPONSIBILITY FOR YOUR OWN CONFIDENCE.

A foundational habit that supports all the emotional work I am describing here is becoming responsible for boosting your own confidence. When you are confident, your bullets trigger you less and you are in more control of your own actions. Also, being more confident will naturally make you a more attractive man. There are chapters coming up that will give you strategies for managing your confidence. You cannot do emotional work without managing your confidence; otherwise, you will simply feel your way into a deep pity party. Ideally, you should engage in any emotional work with high confidence, so after you do the work that drains your confidence, you then you boost your confidence back up and move forward with your day.

6. CLARIFY YOUR TERMS.

Another vital strategy in Stage One is to become crystal clear with knowing and implementing your *terms*. Terms are the only thing in the relationship that you control. Only you can violate your terms, so there is no room for blaming her for anything about your terms. If you try to control anything outside of your terms, you will be endangering your relationship. There is an upcoming chapter that will help you figure out your terms. You need to be rock solid on your terms before leaving Stage One.

7. MITIGATE YOUR NEED TO CONTROL.

Control can feel like safety for a man, but it actually endangers relationships. Instead, the strategy should be to find a space that you can make your own and control the hell out of it. For example: your desk, your half of the garage, a section of your basement, your car. Make it clean and make it yours. This is not meant to create new arguments, so control it without saying a word. If she puts something in the space, simply move it when she's not looking. The rest of your house, however, you don't control. Treat it as if you are a guest and give up the control and criticism about the rest of it all.

Once you have implemented these strategies, you will have brought a level of safety and stability into the relationship. Then, you can then begin to rebuild trust and consistently show her the new man that you are becoming. That is the work of Stage Two.

5
SHE SAYS, "YOU'LL NEVER CHANGE!"

Remember your high school buddy who was 80lbs overweight? Then after falling out of contact for years, you saw him recently on social media and saw his dramatic weight loss? Yeah, maybe you're right – people don't change.

Remember when you last saw your three-year-old niece a decade ago, and then you just saw her over the holidays, and now she's a teenager! Yeah, maybe you're right – people don't change.

Remember that cute girl from college who was the life of the party, always laughing and smiling? You ran into her the other day in the grocery store and she told you about her divorce after they lost their young son in a car accident. Her days of smiling seem far behind her now. But yeah, maybe you're right – people don't change.

When people say, "People don't change," they are trying to give themselves a sense of security based on predicting the future. Yet the truth is that all people do is change. Scientific studies have found that the cells of the entire human body are replaced every seven years. This means that as a newborn, a 7-year-old and a 14-year-old, you have not one single cell in common. The 40-year-old version of you, who remembers your childhood, has only memories of the past – not one single cell of your current body was present in your childhood.

I am not claiming that change is easy or that everyone puts in the hard work and makes the intentional self-aware changes that they should, but every choice, every day, is always changing us and moving us in a direction.

Let's say that I choose to get up right now from my computer, put on my coat and drive to get a dozen donuts and proceed to eat them all. That is going to change the trajectory of my day, my blood sugar, my sleep patterns, my mood etc. On the other hand, I could go out and get a big, beautiful goat cheese and beet salad and that will also affect my day, my blood sugar, my sleep patterns and my mood. Everything we do is a choice and every choice we make sends us in a direction. And if we don't wake up, we end up where we are headed based on unconscious choices that were ingrained in us long ago.

In the three examples above, there is a big difference between your weight-loss buddy from high school versus your niece becoming a teenager and your bubbly college friend losing her joy. The difference is between life happening to certain people as opposed to a person making a conscious choice to take new actions and change their life. The second option is usually a lot of hard work so many people avoid it.

So do people change? Of course. All the time. Every single moment, people are making life-altering choices.

Do people make intentional choices to face and overcome their pain, trauma, fears and terrible habits? Sometimes. And it is brutal, messy, challenging, difficult work that most would rather avoid.

Will people doubt you and your changes? Yes, some will. Will people cheer you on and believe in your changes? Yes, some will. At the end of the day, don't do it for the cheers or the jeers. You must always have your own internal motivation and make the changes for yourself, for your children and for your grandchildren.

As Tony Robbins says, "If I have a gun to the head of your child, I can get you to do anything. Change is always a result of motivation." So realize that you MUST change because your crappy behaviors have put a gun to your child's head and only your change can save them.

Lastly, there are times that people stay stuck in habits that they desperately want to change. Imagine someone with a bullet hole in their bicep: they are not going to be able to lift a 40lb dumbbell. The reason isn't because they are a weak and feeble person; it's because a bullet has literally taken that ability away from them. So why don't people change, even when they want to? Emotional bullets! Bullets take away their ability to change. That is why the emotional work must be done so that intentional changes can be made.

6
STAGE TWO: RESTORING TRUST

"Trust is a dicey subject, everyone wants to be trusted,
but only a few people are willing to put in the work
to show themselves trustworthy."

– Anonymous

Rebuilding trust felt like a long slow slog. It is the hard work of consistently putting tiny deposits of trust into the relationship bank account. On that same day I was putting arborvitaes in the backyard, my wife came out to see the work at one point. After she expressed her thanks, I asked if I could share something with her. She said, "Go ahead." I said, "I have come to realize that you weren't controlling in our relationship (something I had always accused her of), but I have been projecting on you my own childhood pain from feeling constantly controlled." She looked at me with wide eyes, nodded affirmingly and said, "Thank you for acknowledging that," as tears began to fill her eyes. That was one of the first moments in Stage Two where I began to gain bits of trust.

On Father's Day a few weeks later, I got super-triggered and started to blame and verbally finger point at her over something. It was the first time I had done that in about six weeks in the program. I caught myself mid-sentence and said, "I am triggered. Excuse me, I need to go deal with this, I'll be back." I then went out to the punching bag for 20 minutes and dug out the feelings I was holding in. I came back and explained that I had taken the kids to the spray park earlier that day and sat at the picnic tables with all the other dads who brought their kids and listened to all of them complaining about being divorcees and alone on Father's Day. That had triggered a deep fear of ending up alone and abandoned, and I then had been blaming her and projecting that anger and responsibility onto her, like those other men were all doing to their wives. My wife was quite understanding once I had taken ownership and explained. As I look back, I can see that by owning that I was triggered, then dealing with it responsibly, I actually gained trust rather than losing trust. Being triggered doesn't always diminish trust – you can actually gain trust when you own it and deal with it responsibly.

The Stage Two trust rebuilding process can be anywhere from two months to two years or more. It is impossible to know how long Stage Two is going to take, but with the tools of the program, you will have the best chance to rebuild the trust and move through Stage Two powerfully.

STAGE TWO

Welcome to Stage Two. By now, you have dealt with the pain of the slap, and are ready to work on restoring trust in your marriage. You have dealt with any controlling behaviors and any emotionality, so your wife is beginning to feel safe again and not like she has to run for the hills.

You are not out of the woods yet. She may not be pushing for a divorce anymore, but she probably still thinks it is her best option. Her wording may have mellowed out from "I am divorcing you!" to "I still think divorce is what's best for us."

During this stage, she may still push for separation, but it will be more focused on getting space and clarity, and less about anger. Separation at this point is a tool she is using to manage the relationship; it is a way to get some safe space, to explore her own feelings. It may also be to heighten how much you are missing her, and to keep pressure on you to keep working on yourself.

Your objective in Stage Two is to *demonstrate that you are a good man, husband and father,* so that she can trust you once again. You have let her down and she is hurting and wanting more from you – more than she thinks she will get from you. She wants to make sure that the connection that you two had was real, not just a lapse in judgment she made when she was younger. Your goal here is to become a much stronger husband and father and to be trustworthy as a co-parent and friend. *Stage Two is not about being a romantic partner in any way.* Your aim is to make her feel heard, understood, appreciated and valued, as a person and as a mother. It is critical that you fully restore trust with your wife before you switch gears into pursing her as a woman, which is Stage Three.

In Stage Two, do not ask for dates, bring flowers, ask for alone time together or bring up any relationship conversations. Don't use pet names for her, such as "my dear," "sweetie," or "honey." The huge warning here is this: if you start pursing your wife before you have fully restored her trust, she will likely feel you are just trying to manipulate and control her, to win her back, and disrespecting her need for space. If you do that, you will put yourself back into Stage One and you will have lost trust.

Just because she isn't running for a divorce at top speed, that doesn't mean she is ready to let down her walls and open her heart to you. She needs to know that you are going to take care of her heart and needs, and that her hurts can be healed before you move forward.

Let's jump into understanding trust and how to rebuild it. Trust is divided into two major categories: what she needs to trust about you, and what she needs to trust that you can do.

TO KNOW WHAT SHE NEEDS TO TRUST ABOUT YOU, WE USE THE ACRONYM A.W.A.R.E.

Authentic – You know who you are and are consistent with that (i.e. knowing your terms).

Word – You do what you say, you keep your word and you meet her expectations.

Accountable – She needs to know if you break your word, you will own it, apologize and make it right.

Reliable – She can trust that you rarely break your word, except in strange and unusual circumstances.

Ego in check – She needs to feel that your confidence is high and that you don't take things personally, she doesn't have to babysit your emotions, she doesn't have to walk on eggshells around your feelings and you are not easily offended. Her feeling of emotional safety must come as a higher priority above your fragile ego and triggers.

TO TRUST YOU, SHE MUST FEEL THAT YOU ARE AWARE; THE SECOND THING SHE NEEDS IS TO TRUST YOUR ABILITY TO C.A.R.E. FOR HER.

Compassion – You recognize how challenging it is for her to be around you with all the hurt and distrust that has built up over the years. At this stage it is less important that you understand all of it, but essential that you have compassion for what she is dealing with.

Appreciation – You must be a man who builds her up and shows her appreciation for all the love and work she pours into the family as a woman and mother.

Restraint – You respect her boundaries and management of the relationship. Remember, you are not pursuing her in Stage Two; it is critical that you show restraint.

Empathy – You have the ability to listen without judgment and can mirror back to her some of the feelings she is expressing. The next tool below (HUAV) is very helpful in this regard.

When she gets that you are consistently being AWARE and showing CARE, her trust in you as a man, co-parent and friend will likely recover. Keep in mind that the process of destroying trust in your relationship was probably going on over a long time (unless you smashed it all at once with an affair or some such thing), so be patient with the rebuilding process.

During this stage, you are not only rebuilding her trust in you, but you are also rebuilding your trust in yourself as a man. It's about becoming a truly trustworthy man; it isn't about *convincing* her that you are trustworthy. *If* you become trustworthy, then in time, she will be able to trust you again. But during the trust-building stage, do not make promises or give her expectations. Promises should only be made in the context of the Full Bulletproof Apologies, after you have become reliable at keeping them (we will cover Bulletproof Apologies later in the book).

Other than becoming trustworthy in all aspects of your life, you also will be leading her with the quality of your listening skills and by delivering Bulletproof Apologies. By listening and taking ownership, you will actually be pulling her pain out of her, which will create room for a new relationship to be built. When her pain (her bullets) has been pulled out, she will be able to see the man you have become without her emotions clouding her vision. That's when you will know the journey to restored trust is well underway, at which point you will be facing harder, deeper tests!

HERE ARE THE PRACTICAL STRATEGIES FOR STAGE TWO

1. LISTEN AND BE "THE BOWL."
Anything she has to say, whether critical, mean, speaking of other men, throwing the past in your face etc., you will receive. Be solid, do not defend, retaliate or justify, simply listen and get her to share more. The more she shares, the more poison she is ridding from herself.

2. USE OPEN-ENDED QUESTIONS (OEQS).
These are questions that typically begin with "how" or "what" and

cannot be answered by a simple "yes" or "no." Questions such as: "How did that make you feel?" or "What else did you feel when that happened?" These will lead to more feelings being expressed and greater opportunities for her to feel heard, which leads to more trust. Warning: do not use OEQs as a "technique." OEQs must come from a place of genuine care and curiosity. Come to these conversations with the listening mindset you used to have when you were first getting to know her, when you were dating. If she feels heard, she will test you by sharing more information and the more she is heard, the more trust is restored. Make sure you are patient when listening. If she feels rushed or pushed, it will feel emotionally unsafe for her.

3. HEARD. UNDERSTOOD. APPRECIATED. VALUED. (HUAV)

Heard – What feelings do you hear her expressing through what she is saying? Pay attention to her tone and body language, not just her words. The goal is understanding her feelings, not her thoughts or words. You can use this step to mirror it back to her: "It sounds like you are saying you feel…"

Understood – What is her commitment behind what she is saying? Why is she saying what she is saying? She could be yelling at you about forgetting to take out the garbage, but the commitment behind it is her desire for a clean home for your family. You can find a noble commitment behind *anything* she says, you just have to think creatively. Finding the commitment helps you to not take what she is saying as a personal attack. You can use this step to mirror back to her: "It's awesome that you want the house to be clean for our family; I will work on doing a better job of taking the garbage out." When you mirror her commitment back to her, she will feel deeply understood. She may not even know what her commitment is behind her complaint until you comment on it.

Appreciated – When you acknowledge her feelings, and comment and show support toward her commitment, then the next step is to build her up as a person. That is the Appreciation step. It is important to understand that in Stage Two, you are not building her up as a woman, you are building her up as a friend, co-parent and as a mother. The general rule of thumb is this: *only compliment her in ways in which you would compliment your aunt.* Keep your appreciation at that level only, until you have restored trust completely and are moving into Stage Three: pursuit.

Valued – This step is about expressing to her how her commitment makes you a better man, person or father. For example, the Appreciation step would sound like, "I appreciate that you keep our house clean so the kids have a safe and enjoyable home; you're an awesome mom." On the other hand, the Valued step sounds more like, "I am always inspired to step up and keep this house clean and safe because of your example."

HUAV is a super-powerful tool, especially when your wife is pissed off at you – or anyone else is pissed at you, for that matter. Let's go back to the garbage can example and use all four steps:

Her: "UGH! Look at this. 'Mister Helpful' has forgotten to take out the garbage again. You are such a careless shit."

HUAV response: "Hmm, yeah, I forgot. I own that. It sounds like that really frustrates you." (Listen to her response – possibly a long, ranty vent session. Once complete, respond to her points.) "I love that you are always working so hard to keep our house clean for our family, which is so admirable. I appreciate all that work you do and I want to support you. I also realize that you are always challenging me to be a better father by taking care of these things."

Her: "Yeah... whatever." (Hard eye-roll and confused look on her face. Then she thinks about this interaction for the next three days because it was so surprising and supportive.)

Each of the four HUAV steps should be about one sentence long. Keep it as simple and direct as possible, yet aim to include all four elements for it to be the most impactful.

RAISE YOUR INTEGRITY AND DEAL WITH DISTRACTIONS.

In Stage Two, she will continually be poking at your bullet holes and testing you. It is easy to get emotionally triggered when you are not living your life in integrity, so you need to deal with those areas and remove those distractions. She may poke at you about your eating habits, your messy office, you being late all the time, or not spending time with the children, so get your butt in gear. Eat better, clean your office, be five minutes early and spend time tucking the kids into bed; not only will this demonstrate something to her, but it will reduce the arguments, raise your integrity and move you toward being the man you've always wanted to be.

5. MAKE IT LAST.

Whatever you begin to do in Stage Two for rebuilding trust, expect to do it for the rest of your life with her. Once you put this foundation under your house, it will remain forever. Remember, in Stage Two, you are demonstrating that you are reliable, which means you will be consistent in keeping these new habits forever.

6. BE VIGILANT WITH YOUR WORD.

Only give it when you can keep it. Also make sure that you clarify any expectations she has for you, so that you do not inadvertently let her down. Make sure you are keeping your word to her, even if it means you are spending less time with her. In Stage Two, keeping your word to her is far more important than spending time together.

7. PREPARE YOURSELF BEFORE YOU INTERACT WITH HER.

Make sure that your confidence is high and that you have responsibly let out any emotionality. Imagine that before interacting with her, you are going to be tested and you must be as prepared as if you are going behind enemy lines.

8. DON'T DISCUSS YOUR FEELINGS, WANTS OR DESIRES UNLESS ASKED DIRECTLY.

Stage Two is about rebuilding her trust in you; it isn't about your feelings, wants or desires being met. There won't be a focus on you until Stage Four, when she has recommitted and you are both trying to make the relationship work. For now, you are trying to find your way out of a huge trust deficit, so speaking about your wants in this stage will only dig you further into the hole, not get you out of it. If you need to feel heard, respected or appreciated, call a male friend; don't expect that from your wife.

9. DON'T PUSH FOR ROMANCE PREMATURELY.

You can talk about wanting to rebuild trust to have a good co-parenting relationship or a healthy friendship, but do not talk about a romantic relationship unless she directly asks if you want that.

In summary, Stage Two includes several Full Bulletproof Apologies, a lot of deep emotional work and many OEQs and HUAV sessions. It usually takes *several months or longer* for trust to be fully rebuilt. Be patient and expect the tests to keep getting harder until she feels able to start trusting you fully. Then you can put your focus on rekindling the spark, which is Stage Three.

WARNING: Trying to push into Stage Three or beyond without having fully dealt with Stage Two is relational suicide. Every time you are impatient with rebuilding the trust, you will act needy or controlling and this will set you back into Stage One again – you may even get another slap! Slow down. Be patient. Do the work. Give the Full Bulletproof Apologies. Bring your questions to The Bulletproof Husband tribe. You aren't going to make it through this alone.

A helpful context: When coaching a man in stage two, I often share the idea of him sitting in a diner booth across from his wife and they are in a fierce argument. All of the sudden, he pauses, stands up and sits down on her side of the booth. He points across the table and begins to say what she what just saying, "You are such a jerk, I can't believe that you would...." Of course she would be shocked in this scenario. And that is exactly how your newfound tools of empathy, HUAV, and OEQs will come across. Get on her side of the table, it changes everything.

7

ARE YOU GOING TO PLAY THE VICTIM FOREVER?

Imagine that you are extremely overweight. It would be easy for you to point the finger and say, "It's the fast food industry's fault! They put so much salt and sugar in their food that I became addicted! It's my parent's fault because they didn't teach me to eat healthy, nourishing food as a child! The government is to blame because they don't control the size of the meals and drinks I order at the restaurant! It is the system's fault and I am oppressed!" This example may seem absurd, yet a high percentage of people live their life this way. The constant casting of blame upon others and finding fault in everyone else's actions is really just playing the victim.

The victim mindset is the opposite of being responsible and having agency in your own life. If you are only 40% responsible in your life, then you are 60% a victim. Simply put, there is a sliding scale and you get to decide where you are at on the scale. If you take only 20% responsibility for your physical health, then you will be an 80% victim of your careless eating choices, your lack of exercise and being tired and discouraged. Even high achievers and athletes can have an off day that comes from only taking 95% responsibility and casting blame or finding fault in something outside themselves.

When you take 100% responsibility, it doesn't mean that you are the source or cause of everything that has ever happened to you – that would be victim blaming. Yes, terrible things happen: rape, molestation, domestic violence, car accidents, tsunamis, etc. Taking 100% responsibility doesn't mean that you were the cause, that you are to blame, or that it was your fault. Taking responsibility gives you the mindset of owning your situation rather than being a victim of your situation.

Let's say that life handed you two 30lb kettlebells and required you to carry them three miles down the road in the blazing sun, or else something horrendous would happen to your children. Now of course you would have the motivation as a father to get up and get to work. The only real choice in front of you at that point would be whether you were going to moan and complain about how you were a victim of this circumstance or whether you were going to take ownership of the current situation and make the best of it.

You could walk those three miles as a miserable victim, because "Boohoo, this isn't fair. Life isn't supposed to be this way. I can't believe my wife isn't helping; this is half her fault anyway." Or you could decide, "I love my kids; I will do anything to take care of them. I will embrace the suck and take ownership of this situation. These are now my kettlebells to carry and I am not looking for anyone to blame here. I chose to have these kids, and that came with this responsibility now in front of me."

The sliding scale options in front of you are: either be a victim to some degree, or be responsible and take ownership to some degree. The way the scale works, even if you are being 99% responsible in your life (which is extremely rare), you are still being 1% a victim.

Anywhere that you take ownership, you are taking leadership.

Perhaps you decide that you are going to keep your house immaculately clean at all times so that no matter when someone stops by, your house is ready for guests. This is a high level of ownership. It doesn't mean that you must be the one cleaning your house every day. As the one taking ownership, it may mean that you hire a housekeeper to come two days a week to take care of all the housework, or that you enroll your children into daily chores and allowances, etc. Taking ownership is stepping into leadership, yet your personal plate may not have room for you to personally clean the house every day. You can still take ownership and make it happen.

What does this have to do with being masculine and fixing your marriage? Everything!

Most wives feel blamed for giving their husband the slap. When she gave you the slap, she was essentially saying that she had been bearing all the responsibility in the relationship and she wasn't going to anymore. She was demanding that you step up and take responsibility and ownership of your life and become a leader; become the knight in shining armor that she fell in love with. She wanted you to fix her white castle dream that you broke. She had been depending on you and waiting on you to be a responsible leader and take ownership, but instead you blamed, defended, played the victim, argued, hid, made excuses, and all the other cowardice that caused her to lose all hope and respect for you. She hated your bullets and she wanted you to hate them too, to own them, and finally get rid of them.

Until you die, you will always have a chance to take ownership and be responsible. And the best-case scenario is that you lead your family into a new trust-filled relationship. This will require that you always reject the temptation to be the victim and that you take full 100% responsibility, like a masculine man.

When you take 100% responsibility in any area, your wife will feel safe in that area, and safety translates into trust and love for the feminine. If you change your nutrition and exercise habits and get fit, healthy and strong, over time your wife will feel safer and more trusting about your health habits. She won't be nagging you about eating your veggies or going to the gym, because you are light years beyond that and have already proven yourself by owning those areas. Knowing that she is married to a man who is responsible for his health is a turn-on to the feminine because it makes her feel protected and cared for. The same is true for all domains. If she sees you owning your finances, it isn't the pieces of paper with Benjamin Franklin on the front that turn her on, it is the feeling of provision and safety that are provided by your level of responsibility and ownership.

The bottom line is that women do not desire *perfect* men, they desire *responsible* men. And responsible men are rarer to find than ever.

8
STAGE THREE: PURSUIT

*"Inaction breeds doubt and fear. Action breeds con-
fidence and courage. If you want to conquer fear,
do not sit around and think about it. Go out and get
busy."*

Dale Carnegie

I showed up at the house with a dozen roses, a handwritten card and wearing a nice outfit, and was nervous as all get-out. She had agreed to go out with me for dinner for our anniversary. We were still separated at the time, and I had been in solid Stage Two for a couple months at this point. We had a lovely evening and the night ended with the first kiss in ages. Over the coming weeks and months, she would invite me to stay after the kids were put to bed and we'd watch TV together. Depending on where her heart was at, sometimes she would put her head on my shoulder, or sometimes she would build a Great Wall of pillows between us (haha, for real!). I came to understand that pursuing is a part of being the leader of the relationship, but letting her manage means she will either follow your lead or redirect the interaction. Either way, building her up and making her feel desired is what pursuing looks like. It's less about particular actions and more about giving her the feeling of being desired.

STAGE THREE

The journey to Stage Three is a long one and for you to arrive here, you have already become a different man to the one she slapped all those months ago. She is now able to see you as a friend and co-parent, a man who she can trust and rely on, a man who is emotionally solid for her and has taken ownership of the past. Her fears of you going back to being that same old asshole again are starting to fade away and she is beginning to see that a future together might be possible. Now is the time to re-ignite desire within the relationship.

Before we go further into Stage Three, you must read the following warning again: if you begin to pursue your wife romantically before you have fully restored trust with her, she will likely feel controlled and manipulated; you are disrespecting her choice and she will push you back into Stage One!

So moving forward with this chapter, it is dependent on the fact that you have restored her trust in the relationship and are ready to pursue your wife. By doing the work in Stage Zero to the end of Stage Two, you have essentially moved the relationship back to ground zero. So, for example, if you walked up to a woman in a bar and asked for her phone number, you would be starting at Stage Three, and that's normal, but because you have created a massive trust deficit with your wife, you've had to work your way back to the relationship starting line of Stage Three. This is important to recognize because you wouldn't walk up to that beautiful stranger and slap her ass, so keep in mind that although you may have been married for decades, you are going to walk through Stage Three step by step. Don't overstep your wife's physical boundaries in Stage Three – remember, she manages the relationship.

In Stage Two, your focus was on being consistent and reliable. In

Stage Three you will be focused on spontaneity, unpredictability and playfulness. You will be experimenting and then expanding when she accepts you more and more. "What does this look like?" you may ask. Well, it begins with prolonged eye contact, then reaching out to hold hands, then kisses on the cheek or forehead, then intimate kissing, cuddling, and second base, third base and homeruns.

At each step, you will be leading by going 90% of the way and then waiting for her to go 10%. If she doesn't reciprocate, then be confident and playful: perhaps make a silly joke, brush off the rejection and move on.

If she does reciprocate: awesome! Keep playing at that level and next time, try dipping your toes in further. Warning: if you go 100% of the way all at once, you are withdrawing from the trust account and she will feel controlled. This will push you backward in the stages.

In Stage Three, your goal is not to state your own desire – your goal to build *her* desire, and it is also to make her *feel desirable*. Most of her attraction toward you comes from her feeling attractive within herself. It is like you pour a bunch of desirability into her cup and then she needs an outlet to pour it out. When she feels safe and trusts you, you can be that outlet!

Make sure you keep building her up as a woman. Making her feel desirable is the fastest way forward in this stage.

To be in Stage Three, you need to be in solid control of your emotions. Most of your attempts at pursuit will be rejected and you must be able to handle that. Her ability to reject you gives her a confidence boost and makes her feel desired and free. It is also a way in which she is testing you for controlling or needy behavior. If she feels like she needs to nurture you or manage your feelings, it will actually kill the attraction in the relationship because it will pull out her inner mother and not the sexual goddess side, which you are trying to engage. She needs to feel you are confident and can handle rejection with playfulness.

Pursing your wife is something you will be doing throughout Stage Three, Four and Five, and ideally for the rest of your lives together, so if you start winning, don't get complacent – this is ongoing work.

STRATEGIES FOR STAGE THREE

1. SHOW LEADERSHIP THROUGH LISTENING.

In Stage Two you learned to use HUAV when listening to your wife. In that stage you built her up as a friend and mother of your children. In Stage Three you will dig deeper and build her up as a woman, and later as a lover.

2. BE UNPREDICTABLE.

In Stage Three, your pursuit should not be predictable. Remember the example of the woman in the bar you got a phone number from? You wouldn't start that relationship by going out to dinner and a movie every single Friday and bringing her the same bouquet of roses every Sunday – that would be dumb and boring. Instead, you would take her out dancing one week, horseback riding another week, on a picnic another week, etc. Date nights aren't even the best place to start in Stage Three – simply start with compliments, small gifts and other thoughtful ideas that don't ask for much from her. Warning: don't give large gifts too soon into Stage Three. This can easily feel like you are trying to buy her love.

3. AVOID ENDEARMENTS.

Calling her by pet names such as "sweetie," "sweetheart," "honey," "my dear," etc., are for Stage Four, not Stage Three. The woman at the bar who just gave you her number: you aren't going to be the weirdo who starts calling her "my dear" right away, right? Yikes.

4. KEEP IT PLAYFUL AND FUN.

One of the biggest gifts a man can give is making her laugh, and that's also one of the best ways to pursue her.

5. DEMONSTRATE CONFIDENCE THROUGH FLIRTING AND BRAVADO.

Playful overconfidence works. Try it.

6. USE PHYSICAL CONTACT.

Take the opportunity to expand the level of touch between you. The key here is going 90% and let her go the last 10%.

7. GO WITH THE FLOW.

All the strategies here are about the gradual approach. At some point in the process, she may simply surrender and take down all the walls between you. Initially, she may "help" herself surrender by having a glass of wine or by using other methods to relax herself. If she surrenders herself and "goes for you," the 90% rule is out the window. Go with it confidently. If this happens, enjoy it, but don't get expectations or tell yourself some delusional story about how you have reached a new level in the relationship. Go back to the gradual pursuit until she guides you otherwise.

8. BE VIGILANT ABOUT YOUR EMOTIONS.

If you don't handle any of her rejections very well, take note of them. If that is the case, go pull that bullet. Get better with every rejection – she is doing you a favor and helping you find your bullets. And remember, in the beginning, nine out of ten pursuits will end in rejection. Expect rejection and thrive in it, knowing that even her rejecting you is building her up by making her feel more desirable.

9. WATCH FOR THE PUSH AND PULL.

Especially in Stage Three, she will operate in a feminine dynamic that we refer to as the "push and pull." She may accept your pursuit and go out on a date night with you, and she may even make your bed rock afterward. But then, the next morning, it feels like a switch has been flipped and she may act super-cold toward you. Don't take this personally and don't try to fix it. She lives by her feelings and she has to try each feeling on. While she is doing that, she is testing for herself where she should land and where she stands with you in the relationship.

One moment it may feel like she is super-hot for you and the next moment, she is the iceberg that sunk the Titanic. This is good! This is the feminine. If she were solid, consistent and reliable, then she would be in the masculine, and you don't want her in her masculine in Stage Three. So know this: if you are in Stage Three, you can almost set your watch by the push and pull. If she pulls you in, know that she will very soon push you away, and if she is pushing you away, keep pursuing and she will shift soon. The push and pull are very similar to tides in the ocean, it's predictable and you don't need to take it personally. It's just part of the feminine.

10. DON'T PLAY YOUR WHOLE HAND.

Lastly, in Stage Three you should not be discussing your relationship objectives. If she asks you directly if you are trying to seduce her, simply let her know that you are appreciating her more and expressing it at a higher level, now that you have become a more trustworthy man.

Each time your wife surrenders and takes down her walls, she is taking a step further into Stage Three. She may start sprinkling endearments into her communication and being more relaxed around you. She may begin to relabel the relationship as "dating," "a couple," or even "back together." These can be signs that the relationship is getting close to Stage Four.

Entering Stage Four is an aspect of management of the relationship and comes from *her*. Don't push or try to initiate Stage Four, just be consistent in progressing through Stage Three.

If she asks you directly about wanting a committed relationship, then definitely be honest with her about your desire for that. But she is the one who initiates that happening.

WARNING: Do not get ahead of yourself. Only step into Stage Three when you have rebuilt trust.

Here is a helpful context I kept in mind during Stage Three. Let's imagine that your wife has had a beautiful vintage car that she has driven around for 15 years and one day she has to take it into the repair shop. The repairman says, "Your car is dead. It's going to cost $8,000 to replace everything under the hood or you could take that money and try your luck on a used car. If you pay the $8,000, I can guarantee that everything in the new engine is going to be amazing, and you will have the car back that you have loved for 15 years, or you can gamble and take the risk on some other used car that you could find out is garbage and dies on you in three months." Most wives actually want the man they have been with for 15 years to change the engine under the hood and become a solid healthy man. It is an obnoxious amount of work and trouble to go out and find a new man and hope he doesn't turn out to be an asshole like her first husband. So do the work, restore the engine, become a solid man, and know that you have an advantage, especially if you have children together – she wants the father of her children to become a wonderful man.

9
STAGE FOUR: COMMITTED TO A NEW RELATIONSHIP

"Marriage is not a noun, it's a verb. It isn't something you get. It's something you do. It's the way you love your partner every day."

– Barbara De Angelis

About two weeks after she invited me home to stay in the guest room, we had a conversation on the back patio. Even though I was home, I didn't know yet if she was recommitted to the relationship. It was in that conversation that she clearly stated: "If you continue to be this man and don't go back to how you used to be, then I want to be married to you forever. If you go back to how you used to be, I'm out." That was when we stepped into a recommitted relationship.

STAGE FOUR

Stage Four is a huge achievement; she has finally invited you back into being a committed couple. Make sure you take time to look back and celebrate all the changes you have made and the man that you have become!

At this point your wife has decided to give being a couple another try. This will be a longer test for you, and it doesn't mean she is ready yet to surrender the rest of her life to you. The nature of this stage is that she wants to see that you won't get complacent and go back to being an asshole again, now that you have her. She wants to see that not only are you a better man, but that you can consistently be that better man in a relationship with her.

The major shift in Stage Four is that you are *both* trying to make the relationship work. Conversations about the relationship will be more common and, in this stage, can actually be initiated by you. She will continue to test you as she must still get to know the new you, but her reactions in Stage Four are not a rejection of the relationship – they are geared toward improving the relationship.

In Stage Four, your wife will also become your best relationship coach through her management. During this stage, you need to reinforce to her that she is special and cherished, and that she is the woman that you choose forever.

In Stage One you removed codependency, then in Stage Two and Three you became self-sufficient and independent, and now, in Stage Four, you become interdependent. Being interdependent is when two whole, independent individuals decide to depend on each other in specific ways. The difference with these dependencies is that you don't *need* her for you to be a complete, successful and great man. It is a profound truth to be able to say, "I love you, I want you, I choose you, but I don't need you." Now that isn't specifically a romantic statement to make, and won't warm the hearts of the codependents of the world, but it is a healthy and powerful statement to be able to say about yourself in a relationship.

In both Stage Four and Five, a helpful metaphor is that the relationship is about enjoying the journey of dancing through life together. She will want to know that you are solid and self-sufficient enough to get any woman, but on the flip-side of that, she is the only woman for you. She will feel safe knowing that you are a good man who would be successful without her, but that you are the love of her life and desire only her.

In Stage Four, there is a much deeper dance between the masculine and feminine in the relationship. She will feel safe enough to operate more fully and consistently in her feminine and you will be consistently leading from your masculine.

STRATEGIES FOR STAGE FOUR

1. MAKE SACRIFICES AND GESTURES.

She is the one guiding the relationship to the greatest version of health, so during this stage, you will need to be open to making sacrifices and fulfilling her requests. For example, she may want you to give up a certain female friendship or a certain asshole male friendship, going to the bar or watching porn. These are all possible sacrifices on the table. She will guide you in what the relationship needs, but remember, you should never give up your terms.

2. SURPRISES CAN BE BIGGER.

Remember, in the strategies for Stage Three, you were cautioned against large gifts because it could come across as trying to buy her love. Well, now in Stage Four, you can move onto bigger gifts because the relationship is now more secure.

3. STAY CONSISTENT.

Everything you learned in Stage Two and Three continues in Stage Four. Keep using OEQs, HUAV, and being solid, consistent and reliable, and make decisions with the *four priorities* (which we will cover in a later chapter).

4. WORK OUT AREAS FOR RENEGOTIATION.

As commitment grows in the relationship, things from Stage One can be renegotiated. For example, discussions around finances and living arrangements will be back on the table.

5. BE HONEST ABOUT YOUR FEELINGS.

Be open and available to discussing what is going on in your inner world. You can even tell her about things that hurt you or make you angry, but do not express anger to her – you must still deal with that on your own.

6. COMMUNICATE ISSUES THEN TRUST.

If something in the relationship isn't working well for you, share it with her. Share it without expectation or judgment and then trust her to manage it from there.

7. SPEND TIME ON YOUR FOURTH PRIORITY.

You will learn about the top *four priorities* in a later chapter, but in brief, they are the following:

1. Terms
2. Cooperating with her management of the relationship
3. Purpose
4. Wants and desires

In Stage Four, make sure that you are actually putting time and value into your fourth priority, once the other three are being taken care of. Although men who don't ever give time to their wants and desires are men who enable their wives, these men are people pleasers, which means they build up layers of resentment from not valuing themselves.

8. ASK FOR HELP IF YOU NEED IT.

Allow her to contribute to you. When you are struggling, ask her for help. Contribution is an essential part of a relationship and she actually wants to feel helpful and contribute to you. You must be past any weak or stupid bullets that get in the way of allowing her to help you. Ask for her help, input and partnership, but expect nothing. Keep your ability to handle rejection strong, then whenever she does contribute, show appreciation for it and build her up.

When all the commitments and vows have trickled back into your relationship, then ideally, you will be forevermore in Stage Five: "happily ever after." Be sure to never go back to being that complacent, self-absorbed, insecure asshole ever again.

If you find old habits sneaking back in, do a Spot Apology, pull the bullets that are driving the behavior, and then give a Full Bulletproof Apology. Also stay vigilant and ensure you are being responsible, trustworthy, giving appreciation and keeping your expectations in check in the relationship.

Lastly, stay aware of her feelings and make sure you are creating an emotionally safe environment for her to feel heard, understood, appreciated, valued, free, special and cherished. Keep these alive and you will enjoy the marriage you could only dream of having, back when this journey began with the slap.

WARNING: Be vigilant, never complacent. Keep leading. Stay connected to your tribe of men.

Lastly, many men will ask, "Why even get in a committed relationship if it is going to require so much work?" There are three main reasons: 1) It is the best environment to raise children in, 2) to have a good woman that triggers you and helps you find all your wounds so that you can responsibly deal with them and become the best version of yourself, 3) to enjoy the feminine sparkle and shimmer.

10
STAGE FIVE: HAPPILY EVER AFTER

One of the main differences I saw between Stage Four and Five was my wife's bullets. Up to the beginning of Stage Five, I was working on pulling my bullets and getting rid of my triggers. Once my wife had worked through her own wounds and triggers, we were in Stage Five. Stage Five is when she has dealt with her bullets. In our case, she would literally say, "The feelings I am having right now are not your fault, they are my hurts from the past and I am going to need to work through that with my counselor; please just be patient with me."

STAGE FIVE

The nature of Stage Five is that the marriage is no longer in doubt. Your assholery and the broken trust that led to the slap have been forgiven, and she's moved forward with being fully committed to the marriage. The journey from Stage Four to Five was all about working out how to work well together and fully reveal yourselves and accept each other. Stage Five is about keeping that acceptance and trust alive as you grow together.

STRATEGIES FOR STAGE FIVE

1. KEEP VIGILANT ABOUT ALL ASPECTS OF EARNED TRUST.

These are the trusts you started earning in Stage Two. When trust is broken, do a Spot Apology and soon after that, do the emotional work to deal with the bullet and fully restore the trust. Dealing with bullets and showing up in ways that restore trust are a lifelong journey. Inevitably, trusts will be broken at times – the key is to honor your bond of trust in the marriage, and be quick and vigilant about restoring it.

2. GIVE HER THE BENEFIT OF THE DOUBT IN YOUR TRUST FOR HER.

From time to time, she will screw up too – your job is to keep relating to her as your full partner. So, she can't screw up without you also taking responsibility for fixing the screw-up. What lesson can you take away? How quickly can you go back to fully trusting her and giving her the benefit of the doubt? And how quickly can you let her know that your view of her has been fully restored?

3. CHERISH WHO SHE IS AND GIVE SPACE FOR HER HUMANITY.

By the time you've gotten to Stage Five, you should have a pretty good idea about what triggers her and what reactions it prompts from her. Your role is to accept that this is a part of her, and for you to keep giving her space for the areas she is still working through. There are always two parts to someone being triggered – someone has a trigger, and someone pulls the trigger. Make sure you stay generous by not pulling her triggers, but also give her room to grow. This needs to be done in communication with her so you're not being overly helpful or controlling, but are coming from a place of generosity and responsibility.

4. KEEP EXPANDING YOUR ABILITY TO GIVE HER ATTENTION WHEN DESIRED.

She will bid for your attention as a way to feel safe in the relationship. Keep growing in the level of expertise you bring to your terms, so that you can respond as fully and attentively as possible to as many of her bids as possible. You must still keep your terms as priority one, but keep working to minimize their impact on the two of you cooperating.

5. KEEP THE FIRE ALIVE.

Attraction in marriage means bringing polarity. Intentionally bring masculinity to her femininity. Be willing to play those roles even if it isn't who you'd normally be. A big part of keeping attraction alive is uncertainty and danger. Be willing to stretch outside the comfort zone that comes with certainty and acceptance to add that needed spice. Manipulation, control, danger and assholery are all fair game, as long as you both know and agree with the parameters you are setting for these, to ensure they remain inside of the context of intimacy (e.g. "50 Shades of Gray").

6. HAVE ACCOUNTABILITY STRUCTURES.

These must be in place for both your integrity and your confidence around your marriage. The problem with both is that you lack integrity and confidence in the relationship, you're the one least likely to notice. And it was likely that lack of integrity and confidence primarily behind you getting the slap in the first place. Unfortunately, she may not notice when you are slipping in either area, or else she may not have a safe way of communicating it to you. It is vital to keep men in your life. The trap of only relating to your family is you forget that the thoughts you have as a man are normal and natural and you lose acceptance for yourself. Keep connected with your men, in order to keep confident and be vigilant about your integrity.

7. YOU WILL BOTH CHANGE AS YOUR LIVES EVOLVE.

Be each other's witnesses, sounding boards, champions and safety nets. Be open to her surprising you from time to time, and sometimes how she changes can shake up your life. Never get entitled or complacent with how important she is for you, or how hard it was to restore that broken trust with her in the past.

8. KEEP RELATING TO HER AS YOUR PARTNER.

As fears, doubts, hurts, jealousies, external desires or anything else comes up, let her know and trust her to be your partner through it. Once again, give her the benefit of the doubt – she's likely much stronger than you give her credit for. She has accepted you as you are, and you are sharing your journey together through all of it. She could likely be a huge help as you face these challenges.

SECTION RECAP

- The slap: Embrace it, you needed it, this is going to change you for the better.
- Stage Zero: Grieve, cry, rage, wail, get the pain and hurt out.
- Stage One: Remove all control, let her be as if she had already divorced you.
- Stage Two: Use all the tools for rebuilding trust, settle in for the long slog, build and deliver your Full Bulletproof apologies.
- Stage Three: Begin to dip your toe in pursuit; remember the 90/10 rule.
- Stage Four: Don't get complacent; ensure your masculine tribe keeps you accountable.
- Stage Five: Design a new relationship as two new people.
- Why do all this? Your children need you to step up as a leader and lead the relationship out of the ditch you lead it into.
- Do people actually change? Yes. With intention and focused effort, you can make profound changes.

MEMBER STORY: FROM ALMOST DEAD TO FULLY ALIVE

I've been a bullet-riddled asshole for as long as I can remember. The mad-at-the-world, take-it-out-on-everyone, miserable bastard that wasn't happy unless I was projecting my misery onto everyone around me, kind of asshole. Then fate happened and I met a very wonderful girl in November of 1988. We quickly fell in love because she saw something I never saw in myself. I never understood why she loved me, but I hated myself, and quickly resented her for it.

We married on June 29th, 1991 and had our first son on January 8th, 1993. I was not ready to be a father and this caused my bullets to just explode. The stress was unbearable and I buried myself in work just so I didn't have to deal with it. We had another son in 1995 and he was an easy baby. However, my oldest son began emulating me, bullets and all, and what he didn't know was how much I truly hated myself. When I saw my traits arise in him, I hated him too. By now we had a third son, I was much older and it was a chance to redeem myself for not being there for my other boys. Nevertheless, the damage was done and constant fights between my oldest son, my wife, and me took their toll, and about six years ago my wife hatched a plan to go to RN school so she could sustain herself and divorce me.

On November 15th, 2019 she couldn't take it any longer, slapped me, packed some clothes and left to live with a girlfriend of hers. This is the first time she actually left. She had threatened a bunch of times over the 28 years we were married, but had never followed through. I realized I'd truly messed up. I also realized for the first time how much hurt I caused on the people I was supposed to be loving. It was soul crushing. I found TBH and booked a breakthrough call and spoke to Endre on November 29th 2019 and entered the program. My wife signed a year lease the following month on a rental.

I quickly got involved and searched the modules for the "magic bullet" that would fix my marriage. For about six weeks, I was bullshitting myself into believing that I was doing this for me. I wasn't, and she saw right through it. Her mother fell ill in mid-January and she needed my help so I was able to coordinate that. Because we were getting along, I wrongly attached the expectation that things were getting better and we were getting back together. Also, all of my wins were biased entirely on her. Her mother passed away and after the funeral my wife ghosted me for about two weeks. I slipped into major depression. A few guys tried to talk me off the ledge but I wouldn't listen to reason.

I muddled through February 2020 not doing any TBH work, not talking to other men, not posting on Facebook, and doing nothing but wallowing in self-pity. After she ignored my birthday – the best birthday present she gave my co-dependent needy ass – I hit rock bottom. I saw some wins posted by other members and thought, "These guys are winning, what the hell am I doing wrong?"

It was early March 2020 and one night I had a shotgun under my chin and was about to end all the misery. My son came home from work and when I heard him come in the front door, I decided not to end it all. I decided that I was done feeling sorry for myself and decided to do this work for myself. I got on a Monday night call, called myself out on my bullshit, and declared I was doing the work for myself to the tribe. I figured I had nothing left to lose anyway. In August of 2020, Endre sent me a message inquiring if I'd be interested in becoming a member coach. I jumped at the opportunity!

A month later my wife moved back home and we've been happily ever after ever since. I continue to do the work required to sustain a bulletproof way of life. When I slack off, I backslide. She notices immediately and will tell me. There's no ego – I'm just thankful to have her watching my blind spots and willing to keep me moving forward. My wife has become my best life coach.

This program and the men in the tribe saved my life.

NON-TOXIC MASCULINITY

11
THE MACHO MAN

remember being 17 years old and longing to understand how to become a "man." I reached out to older men from my church and would pick their brains about what "being a man" meant to them. I was hungry for a clear definition, to simply, clearly understand what is masculine and how to live and feel masculine. I never got the clarity I was looking for and rather than feeling solid and anchored in my masculinity, I was adrift at sea and caused a lot of damage until I found my way to The Bulletproof Husband. If you have gotten the slap, I would be willing to bet that you never got a clear definition that anchored you in your masculinity either.

To even have a discussion nowadays regarding masculinity requires that I begin by saying what I am *not* referring to as masculine. Here are five clarifications:

1. Being masculine doesn't mean that you are an arrogant, selfish asshole. That comes from being a deeply wounded person, not a masculine person.
2. Acting macho or tough is not the same as being masculine. You can hunt, fish, carry a pocketknife at all times, do martial arts and listen to "The Joe Rogan Experience" and still not be masculine – in fact, you can do all those things and have a vagina.

3. Being masculine doesn't mean that you are socially unacceptable. It doesn't mean that you are impolite, constantly swear, burp, fart and have bad hygiene. For example, think of James Bond – a truly masculine character, yet extremely refined.

4. Being masculine doesn't mean that you are emotionally unavailable, distant and aloof. Those are characteristics of a trauma response, not masculinity.

5. Masculinity isn't just related to being male. Women can be in their masculine side at times and men can be in their feminine side at times. Masculinity and maleness often go together, yet they are not synonymous.

Now that we have looked at what masculinity isn't, let's define the masculine and feminine. To understand the masculine clearly, it is best to contrast it with its polar opposite, the feminine. Although they are opposites, that doesn't mean they are in opposition to each other. The feminine isn't the same as the anti-male feminist. Masculine and feminine are contrasting in the same way that north and south magnets are opposites, yet those opposing magnets are actually drawn toward each other. The more that a man is in his masculine and a woman is in her feminine, the more opposite they will be, yet also the more attracted and magnetized they will be to each other. When a man and woman are both being masculine or both being feminine, they actually repel each other like two north magnets or two south magnets. Simply stated, the masculine and feminine are opposites: they attract each other and they are complimentary.

To more clearly define the nature of the masculine and feminine, a metaphor is helpful. In The Bulletproof Husband, we use the bowl and the water for a clear understanding. The masculine bowl is simple, solid, consistent, steady, reliable – it's just a plain bowl on the table. Conversely, like water, the feminine can be still and peaceful in the bowl, it can splash, it can evaporate into a mist, it can freeze solid, it can boil, it can have a beautiful sparkle or it can be a hurricane.

This depiction is timeless. We can see this whether we look at the Hindu Vedas' depiction of the masculine Shiva and feminine Goddess Kali, or the Taoist Ying and Yang, the Judeo-Christian Holy Spirit as the feminine aspect of God with God the Father as the masculine aspect, or even how Dr. Jordan Peterson describes chaos (feminine) and order (masculine) in "12 Rules for Life." All of these cultures give a depiction of the masculine and feminine that is similar to the bowl and the water. Unfortunately, the modern Western world has become deeply disconnected from the ancient understanding of the masculine and feminine, and as a result, our entire culture and marriages have been missing this ancient wisdom.

Here are a few insights that come from recognizing the distinction of masculine and feminine.

The feminine is always testing the masculine to make sure it is solid and reliable. This looks to a man like she is picking fights and trying to irritate him for no reason. Yet there is a reason. The feminine is always checking for safety, and a triggerable man is not a safe man (more on this in the chapter entitled "Why Is She Being Such a B*tch?").

The masculine is guided by his terms, then by cooperating with her management of the relationship, then his purpose and lastly by his feelings and wants. The feminine is guided by being true to her feelings. If a man is letting his feelings guide his decisions, he is being feminine. We see this every day in The Bulletproof Husband: before a man knows his terms or how to do emotional work, he will be guided and dominated by his feelings. That is a terrible place to be as a man. It is scary to your woman and causes a ton of damage.

Another difference is how the masculine and feminine handle their feelings. The feminine throughout history has been a part of homemaking in a tribal or village setting. This lends itself to being able to verbally process and emote one's feelings. The masculine has been going out of the village on the hunt, either for a saber-tooth tiger or in war parties against other tribes. These would have been very tense and scary situations, so the masculine has a built-in ability to suppress his feelings until they can be let out later, perhaps in a wild dance around a raging tribal fire. The problem enters the picture when the modern man has no tribal fire, no tribe and is in a gender-neutral world, sitting in a therapist's office trying to talk about his feelings like a girl, when what he really needs is to hit a tire with a sledgehammer, scream his guts out and then cry his face off until he has emptied the emotional tank.

Lastly, as Endre Gabori says, one of the main differences between the masculine and feminine is that "the masculine acts and then feels, whereas the feminine feels and then acts." What does that mean? Let's use sex as an example. When a woman has sex, it is because she first felt loved and opened herself to the masculine, whereas a man is always open for sex, and after the act of sex, he then feels loved. The experience is completely opposite. She needs the foreplay to get the feeling of being desired and once she has that feeling, she is able to step into sexuality, whereas the man can step into sexuality at any moment but afterward will feel connected and loved.

So far this chapter is only laying a foundation for the differences between the masculine and feminine. The rest of this book will go into more detail and application. For now, just know that understanding the masculine and learning how to be the bowl is the most powerful tool for fixing your marriage. I may even be underselling the power of being a masculine man here, but it can make your marriage work, it will put you at peace with yourself, it will cause you to gain the respect of other men and bring you success in life. That's the tip of the iceberg regarding being a masculine man.

SEVEN DEFINING CHARACTERISTICS OF MASCULINITY

1. THE MASCULINE MAN KNOWS WHAT HE TRULY WANTS.

This is deeper than it may seem at first glance. Knowing what you truly want means that you have cleared away the distraction of what you *think* you want. Often the biggest trap for a man is thinking that he wants approval. This leads him to be a pleaser to try to gain acceptance. Ultimately, that means he is trying to change himself for others rather than truly being himself.

Another pitfall men fall into is trying to avoid feeling our own hurt feelings. Rather than truly knowing ourselves and being ourselves, we live as reactions to our past hurts and try to numb them out or avoid ever feeling that way again.

2. THE MASCULINE MAN KNOWS WHAT HE WILL NOT COMPROMISE (HIS TERMS).

When a man truly knows himself, he also knows what he will not compromise. He knows that he cannot compromise on certain things without literally giving up who he is as a person. It would be better for him to give up the marriage than to compromise who he is as a man. Another way to say this is that a masculine man knows his terms and always honors them. The eye-opening thing about terms is that once you know them and stand by them solidly, you will never feel emasculated again. In fact I have met scrawny cubicle dwellers that are more masculine men than the jacked muscular gym dwellers. Masculinity is not about your size and attitude; it is about clarity and ability to not compromise on your terms.

3. THE MASCULINE MAN AMBITIOUSLY PURSUES WHAT HE WANTS.

The masculine is known for taking action. Words are just fairy dust until action is taken. Actions speak louder than words, and actions are to be trusted over words. A masculine man is the leader of his own life and doesn't blame others or the situations in his life. He simply takes responsibility and moves forward.

4. THE MASCULINE MAN KNOWS HIS STRENGTHS AND WEAKNESSES.

To know your strengths is to know where you are competent. You have the ability to give your word about something and fulfill your word. You are able to deliver. If you have competence, which leads to confidence, then you have a strength. If you are not consistent and reliable in producing results in a particular area, then you have a weakness. The masculine man isn't deterred by the fact that he lacks competency in an area. He doesn't try to cover that up and hide that fact from others. That's what the approval-seeking pleaser tries to do. The masculine man is self-aware and accepts himself flaws and all.

5. THE MASCULINE MAN SOLVES PROBLEMS WITHOUT COMPLAINT.

Again, the masculine man does not blame others or the situation; he takes action to deal with the challenge in front of him. In fact, he sees each "problem" in front of him as a "challenge" to overcome.

6. THE MASCULINE MAN IS DECISIVE AND DIRECT.

It is not masculine to get stuck in your head, constantly mulling over what decision to make. The masculine is about taking action. Once the needed information is gathered, then the five-second rule applies. The masculine makes a decision and takes action. Also, the masculine man doesn't dance around sticky subjects with his words. He speaks clearly and directly. Especially since approval isn't the goal – being authentically oneself requires clear, direct communication.

7. THE MASCULINE MAN IS SIMPLE AND EASY-GOING.

Unlike the emotional nature of the feminine, which splashes and changes like water, the masculine is the simple, stable, solid bowl. It sits undisturbed on the table and isn't needy, clingy or emotionally fragile. Another metaphor for this would be couples dancing, such as salsa or tango. The masculine partner is basically there to provide structure for the feminine partner to spin and flourish, sparkle and shine.

I am not saying that masculine men don't have emotions. The masculine man *does* have emotions but he does not let his emotions control his actions and decisions.

12

GOT THAT BIG D*CK ENERGY

There is an extremely common pattern with men who get the slap. They have become dependent on their wife's praise and approval to have any confidence. Here's how that happens: when you were dating, your confidence attracted her to you, but after she committed to the relationship, you gradually stopped managing your confidence and made her responsible for how you feel about yourself. Over time, you have actually taken on the qualities of an addict and are completely dependent on her happiness for you to feel confident within yourself. This state of being is the "happy wife, happy life" phase of being. The truth is that you can be confident and happy, whether your wife is or not! But this will require you becoming responsible for your confidence and proactively managing it with self-awareness.

If you don't take responsibility for your own confidence, you will live in the self-pity and pain of relying on her at the point when she has turned off the supply, leaving you feeling like you are now like a drug addict trying to get sober. You are likely spiraling and looking for any drop of affirmation that you are doing the right thing, etc.

You have to become 100% responsible again for maintaining

your own confidence. Do the work intentionally this time and learn how to manage your own confidence so that you are never at the mercy of someone else's approval or disapproval again. Remember, men take action first and that brings us the feelings. Below are some actions that can be taken which will provide the feeling of confidence.

There are three things you can do to raise your confidence in the short term:

1. **Keep a wins journal.** Have a journal where you write down at least three wins every day. Just by acknowledging even small wins every day, you get into the habit of looking for the things that boost your confidence. This journal can be helpful for going back and reviewing regularly, especially when you are having an "off day" and just need to boost yourself up.

2. **Keep an anger journal.** This is your journal for puking all your ugliest feelings. It's not complicated. Just write and dump this garbage and get it out. You don't need to go back and review the journal, although it may be a helpful reference tool when do intentional bullet-pulling work. Otherwise, make sure that she ABSOLUTELY DOES NOT see this journal. This is for your eyes only.

3. **Have an integrity checklist.** This is similar to having a to-do list. The main difference is that it includes all your unfinished tasks too. This may include how you signed up for an ecourse and never finished it, your friend left you a voicemail and you still haven't called him back, etc. Anything that would be mental clutter or distraction, not simply household to-do items. Every time you accomplish an item on this list, you will feel a boost of confidence, perhaps for 20 minutes if it is a small task, or two weeks for accomplishing a large task.

Here are five things that will raise your confidence in the long term:

1. **Knowing your terms.** Once you have the clarity that comes from knowing who you are and what you will not compromise, this gives you an internal foundation of confidence that you can build your life on top of.

2. **Purpose (outside of marriage).** When you are applying yourself to purposeful work outside your marriage, you will feel that you have a place in this world, a place you belong and have value regardless of how your wife feels about you from moment to moment.

3. **Pulling your bullets.** Each time you pull out a bullet, you are removing insecurity and moving into higher levels of confidence and security. I sometimes picture a man's bullet holes as a thousand tiny doors all over his chest and limbs. As each tiny door is opened it lets out a poisonous green gas that has been trapped within him for decades. Each suppressed emotion that is felt and released moves a man into greater health and confidence naturally.

Following the four-part structure for prioritizing actions. When a man grasps the filtering system for choices:

1. Terms
2. Management of relationship
3. Purpose
4. Feelings

... there is such a clarity that enters his life. That clarity brings confidence.

4. **Context.** When a man is able to reframe any horrible situation into something that will benefit him or

improve his life, he will feel the confidence that comes from life happening *for* him rather than feeling like life is happening *to* him.

THE CONFIDENCE STAIRCASE

Confidence is like being on a spiral slide. Either you are climbing up or you are sliding down. You are rarely standing still at a specific level of confidence. If you take the right actions, you will go up into higher levels of confidence, but if you are not proactive and you let life happen to you, you will begin to slide down into insecurity and instability.

Each time you do actions that boost your confidence, you will feel a sense of competence. That competence is what boosts confidence. Say, for example, you have worked for three months on a project at work and one day, your boss comes and acknowledges all your hard work and gives you a pay rise and a promotion. You go home and your son tells you that he just made the starting line-up for the football team and it's because you have been helping him practice on the weekends. Your wife then announces that it is March 14th and she will be celebrating you this year![3] On a scale of 1-10, your confidence will be at 97! You are a freaking rockstar. And that confidence isn't an accident; it has happened because you have taken ownership in these areas of your life and the competence in these areas has led to these wins and this level of confidence.[4]

3| AKA "Steak and blowjob night" – an unofficial holiday which balances out Valentine's Day.

4| I have used examples here of external wins, yet you can build your confidence through recognizing your internal wins as you will see in the chapters about context. Particularly if you have received the slap, it may be a while before you are having external wins.

13
LONE WOLVES GET SLAUGHTERED

For thousands of years, humanity lived in tribes. Men typically went out for days or weeks at a time in hunting parties, while women stayed in the village, cared for children and gathered nearby plants and berries.

Men were out with other men, doing purposeful work and providing for their families. This continued even up to the Industrial Revolution at the beginning of the 1800s. During the Industrial Revolution, men didn't go off in hunting parties, but they went to work with other men at the construction site or steel mill for brutally long workdays.

Rather than giving a long discourse about how we have gotten to the modern era, I will jump ahead. Suffice it to say that the modern man relates more with the boiling, frustrating malaise depicted in the movie "Fight Club," rather than having a root system of masculine men who he can call his tribe. Rather than being heralded as legends for our honorable acts and deeds, the modern male is labeled as having "toxic masculinity." Yet, that very term is a misnomer, because real masculinity is non-toxic. "Toxic masculinity" refers to the insecure, controlling, manipulative, self-protecting beta-male coward. I can tell you from 35 years of firsthand experience, there is nothing masculine about that way of being. Yes, the toxic man is a male, but that does not mean he is masculine, nor is masculinity his problem; the lack of true masculinity is the problem.

True masculinity is about solidness. A masculine man lives by his principles no matter the cost. He is secure and never tries to control his relationships. He speaks clearly and directly without mincing words. He is stable, consistent, and reliable. He is physically and emotionally a safe place for his family and friends.

The consistently masculine man always has a tribe of masculine relationships that challenge and champion him, a place where he can vent his frustrations and share the celebration of his wins. Being masculine is not about going out to kill the wooly mammoth by yourself; trying to be masculine without a tribe actually comes from insecurity and arrogance. Instead, the masculine man surrounds himself with a tribe that has the balls to look him in the eye and say, "No." "You are wrong." "You are messing up." "Don't do it that way or your wife will divorce you and your kids will resent you." Your tribe must not only have the guts to confront, but then also have the clarity and wisdom to teach you exactly where to step and how to walk the path into masculinity, as well as cheer you on and catch you when you trip.

When you are going through tough times with your marriage, your friends and family are going to be super-biased and they are not going to give worthwhile advice. If you want trustworthy advice, find men who don't know your wife, but have navigated tough times in their own marriage and are willing to listen to you, and lift you up into being a better man and husband. Finding those kinds of men can be very difficult.

Up until my mid-30s, I lived as a toxic beta/Mr. Nice Guy. And although I had friends, family, board members, therapists and many other men who tried to help me and confront me over the years, I would defend myself and argue from my deep insecurity. For some men, perhaps it is easier to find the path to masculinity, yet for those of us who are loaded with bullet holes like I was, it took a very skilled tribe to help me confront my insecurities and lead me where I needed to go within myself to become solid.

Similarly, if you need to lose weight, you are going to need a tribe with a specific kind of insight; if you need to get sober, you need a different tribe; if you need help as the parent of a toddler, you need a different tribe. The challenge you are facing also reveals what kind of tribe you need. When I had humiliated myself internationally, collapsed my ministry, been excommunicated from my local church, had former staff members writing blogs about me, and was facing my own likely divorce, I needed the likes of Endre Gabori, John Scannell and Gary Menezes to gather around me with The Bulletproof Husband tribe, roll up their sleeves and get to work on straightening me out and showing me the way into true masculinity.

It is humbling to realize that you need a tribe and that you aren't getting where you need to all by yourself. But it is exactly that humbling which prompts your first step toward lasting change, whether it is hiring a physical trainer, a dietician or going to a 12-step group, finding your tribe is a life-changing experience. If you are like most men, your life is probably lopsided, and it is time to rebalance your time in the village with family and your time in connection with other masculine men who are out on the hunt.[5] And if your woman has given you the slap, you need a tribe to help you become the truly

5| Can you imagine what would happen inside a man who is constantly at the tribal village, while all the other men are out hunting or at war? By being alone, over time, his masculinity will erode and he will get himself into hot water such as affairs or other schemes, such as the famous story of the ancient King David staying home in Jerusalem while all the other kings and warriors went out to war (2 Samuel 11). This led to him having an affair with his soldier's wife, impregnating her, and then having the soldier killed to cover up the indiscretion; quite the turmoil, and all because the Israelite king was isolated, rather than with his tribe where he belonged.

masculine man that your wife and children have been longing for. [6]

Lastly, regarding having a tribe, I want to share a powerful story from Stephen Mansfield's book "Ten Signs of a Leadership Crash."

> *There is a wonderful African American church that had a wonderful men's ministry because they had a wonderful men's ministry leader named Taylor. This devoted man led that phenomenal group of loving, passionate, adventurous, largely African American men for years. Then something hurtful happened, the kind of thing that occurs in churches when senior pastors change and the new leader has a new direction for the church. So Taylor got hurt. Deeply. And he resigned and left.*

> *He was embarrassed. He didn't know how to process it all. He felt best in isolation. So he locked himself up in his house, he wouldn't answer the phone, he wouldn't see anybody, and he thought he could get through it alone, just Taylor and God. Yet he was not doing well at all.*

> *The hundreds of men in that wonderful men's ministry were disturbed. Thankfully Taylor had taught them to love each other well. They had no intention of letting Taylor go quietly and wounded into the bitter night. So they got permission from his wife and camped out in Taylor's yard. They literally pitched tents, brought in food, and sat around with big signs Taylor couldn't help but see from his windows: "Taylor, we love you," "Talk to us Taylor," "We aren't leaving*

6| A metaphor I often share with men when they join a men's group like Bulletproof Husband is to think of joining a martial arts school. You will be a brand new white belt and it will be tempting to just hang out in the corner with other white belts. Yet the other white belts are brand new and are the most likely to get you hurt! You are going to be far safer if you can team up with a higher belt color, they will teach you and keep you safe. The same is true in a men's program. Find guys that are seasoned and can pour into you. Also find a peer that can relate on the same level and after a little while, find a new guy and begin to pour into him too.

without you," "Taylor, you're an idiot. Get out here."

Did Taylor come out? Nope. He called the police. He was angry. So the police came. Taylor's wife and a few members of the church occupation force told the police what was going on. When the police had heard everything, one of them said, "I wish the folks at my church cared about each other this much. You stay right here until this fool realizes how many people love him." Then the police started patrolling the makeshift camp to make sure that all was well for the campers.

Then the police decided to help. Every day they would stop by Taylor's house, wade through the campers, eat some of the amazing BBQ that the guys were cooking in hopes of "smoking Taylor out," and knock on Taylor's door. Every single day: "Sir, we've been asked to make sure you're okay. We've received calls. Sir, are there any guns in here? Sir, are you alright? Are you in any danger of harming yourself?"

Of course, none of this overzealous policing was necessary but it is legal and it made a point. More importantly, it brought Taylor to the door once a day and this gave the men camping in his yard a chance to shout their love.

Finally, Taylor broke. There were tears, apologies, group hugs and massive amounts of BBQ. All was put right, and why? Because a group of men pursued. They didn't let isolation become the norm. They didn't sit around scratching their heads saying, Whatever happened to ol' Taylor? He was a good guy. Haven't seen him in years." No, Taylor's tribe decided that Taylor was worth pursuing and winning back.[7]

7| Kindle version, pages 18–20.

14
YOUR WORD IS YOUR BOND, PART 1

Having grown up in church, my perspective of "accountability" was meeting with other guys weekly to have coffee and talk about how we were failing at quitting porn. Eventually such accountability always falls apart because who wants to do that every week forever? When I read the following story and learned about integrity from The Bulletproof Husband, it radically shifted my perspective.

Twenty years ago, in Nashville, Tennessee, during the first week of January, 1996, more than 4,000 baseball coaches descended upon the Opryland Hotel for the 52nd annual ABCA Convention.

While I waited in line to register with the hotel staff, I heard other more veteran coaches rumbling about the lineup of speakers scheduled to present during the weekend. One name kept resurfacing, always with the same sentiment

– *"John Scolinos is here? Oh, man, worth every penny of my airfare." Who is John Scolinos? I wondered. No matter; I was just happy to be there.*

In 1996, Coach Scolinos was 78 years old and five years retired from a college coaching career that began in 1948. He shuffled to the stage to an impressive standing ovation, wearing dark polyester pants, a light blue shirt, and a string around his neck from which home plate hung – a full-sized, stark-white home plate.

Seriously, I wondered, who was this guy?

After speaking for 25 minutes, not once mentioning the prop hanging around his neck, Coach Scolinos appeared to notice the snickering among some of the coaches. Even those who knew Coach Scolinos had to wonder exactly where he was going with this, or if he had simply forgotten about home plate since he'd gotten on stage. Then, finally…

"You're probably all wondering why I'm wearing home plate around my neck," he said, his voice growing irritable. I laughed along with the others. "I may be old, but I'm not crazy. The reason I stand before you today is to share with you baseball people what I've learned in my life, what I've learned about home plate in my 78 years."

Several hands went up when Scolinos asked how many Little League coaches were in the room. "Do you know how wide home plate is in Little League?"

After a pause, someone offered, "Seventeen inches?" as more of a question than an answer.

"That's right," he said. "How about in Babe Ruth's day? Any Babe Ruth coaches in the house?"

Another long pause. "Seventeen inches?" came a guess from another reluctant coach.

"That's right," said Scolinos. "Now, how many high school coaches do we have in the room?" Hundreds of hands shot up, as the pattern began to appear. "How wide is home plate in high school baseball?"

"Seventeen inches," they said, sounding more confident.

"You're right!" Scolinos barked. "And you college coaches, how wide is home plate in college?"

"Seventeen inches!" we said, in unison.

"Any Minor League coaches here? How wide is home plate in pro ball?"

"Seventeen inches!"

"RIGHT! And in the Major Leagues, how wide is home plate in the Major Leagues?

"Seventeen inches!"

"SEV-EN-TEEN INCHES!" he confirmed, his voice bellowing off the walls. "And what do they do with a Big League pitcher who can't throw the ball over 17 inches?" Pause. "They send him to Pocatello!" he hollered, drawing raucous laughter. "What they don't do is this: they don't say, 'Ah, that's okay, Jimmy. If you can't hit a 17-inch target? We'll make it 18 inches or 19 inches. We'll make it 20 inches so you have a better chance of hitting it. If you can't hit that, let us know so we can make it wider still, say 25 inches.'"

He paused. "Coaches... what do we do when our best player shows up late to practice? Or when our team rules forbid facial hair and a guy shows up unshaven? What if he gets caught drinking? Do we hold him accountable? Or do we change the rules to fit him? Do we widen home plate?"

The chuckles gradually faded as 4,000 coaches grew quiet, the fog lifting as the old coach's message began to unfold. He turned the plate toward himself and, using a Sharpie, began to draw something. When he turned it toward the crowd, point up, a house was revealed, complete with a freshly drawn door and two windows.

"This is the problem in our homes today. With our marriages, with the way we parent our kids. With our discipline. We don't teach accountability to our kids, and there is no consequence for failing to meet standards. We just widen the plate!"

He paused again. Then, to the point at the top of the house he added a small American flag. "This is the problem in our schools today. The quality of our education is going downhill fast and teachers have been stripped of the tools they need to be successful, and to educate and discipline our young people. We are allowing others to widen home plate! Where is that getting us?"

The crowd was silent. He replaced the flag with a cross. "And this is the problem in the church, where powerful people in positions of authority have taken advantage of young children, only to have such an atrocity swept under the rug for years. Our church leaders are widening home plate for themselves! And we allow it.

"And the same is true with our government. Our so-called representatives make rules for us that don't apply to themselves. They take bribes from lobbyists and foreign countries. They no longer serve us. And we allow them to widen

home plate! We see our country falling into a dark abyss while we just watch."

I was amazed. At a baseball convention where I had expected to learn something about curve balls and bunting and how to run better practices, I had learned something far more valuable.

From an old man with home plate strung around his neck, I had learned something about life, about myself, about my own weaknesses and about my responsibilities as a leader. I had to hold myself and others accountable to that which I knew to be right, lest our families, our faith and our society continue down an undesirable path.

"If I am lucky," Coach Scolinos concluded, "you will remember one thing from this old coach today. It is this: if we fail to hold ourselves to a higher standard, a standard of what we know to be right; if we fail to hold our spouses and our children to the same standards, if we are unwilling or unable to provide a consequence when they do not meet the standard; and if our schools and churches and our government fail to hold themselves accountable to those they serve, there is but one thing to look forward to..."

With that, he held home plate in front of his chest, turned it around, and revealed its dark black backside: "...We have dark days ahead!"

His message was clear: "Coaches, keep your players – no matter how good they are – your own children, your churches, your government and most of all, keep yourself at 17 inches."

15
YOUR WORD
IS YOUR BOND,
PART 2

L et's carry the home plate metaphor a bit further from the previous chapter.

When the baseball pitcher throws the ball within the 17 inches of home plate, let's call that operating within integrity. When he throws it outside the plate, he is out of integrity. If he keeps promising himself that he will throw it over the plate and keeps missing, then his trust in himself is going to diminish. He will know that he is not a man of his word.

Integrity in this sense is not about ethics and morality. It is about keeping your word and being trustworthy. It means if you commit to something, you will follow through, regardless of the cost. And if you cannot keep your word, you will let the other person know before the committed deadline comes up and will do your best to repair the lost trust. For example, if you said you would be somewhere at 7 o'clock, and you see that you are going to be 10 minutes late, you text the other person before you are late, letting them know you are going to be late, and let them know it was your error and you will do 10 pushups to "clean it up."

Our modern culture doesn't expect this of anyone and you will immediately be operating at a much higher level of integrity and accountability. By doing the pushups, you are not stuck in your head beating yourself up for being late, you get out of your head, you make minor amends for the lateness and you get back to being a man of your word. Accountability really works when you follow three simple steps:

1. Make a commitment.
2. Give yourself a consequence for if you don't keep your word.
3. Ruthlessly keep your word or follow through on your consequence (otherwise you will lose trust in yourself and your ability to stay within integrity).

I have several men with whom I keep myself accountable each week, and they do the same. We make goals together and give ourselves consequences, then we follow up on our self-imposed goals and consequences. For example, I might say, "By next Saturday at noon, I will work out four times at the gym or else I will post a wet-T-shirt picture of myself in our private Facebook group."[8] Then I will ruthlessly keep my word. As a tribe of men, we keep making new goals and consequences to keep pushing ourselves further into emotional work, to growth within the domains (we will cover the domains later in the book), and into being the men we have always wanted to be.

I challenge you to use your tribe to step up your own integrity, accountability and to know yourself as trustworthy. The feminine is

---

8| This is simply one example, but there are endless consequences that you can use: cold showers, jumping jacks, push-ups, shaving an eyebrow, singing "I'm a little teapot" on social media, running a mile, etc.

naturally drawn toward the solidness of a trustworthy, accountable, man of integrity, so get to work.

16
WHY DO YOU KEEP FAILING EVERY FOUR WEEKS?

Willpower is closely associated with self-control. Say for example that you have a habit of eating at fast food restaurants and you make a New Year's resolution to eat healthier and lose weight. If you are like the vast majority of people, a couple weeks into the New Year, your willpower is worn out and you are right back to your ingrained habits. When the willpower tank is depleted, self-control is lost.

Willpower in relationships looks like the man trying to push down his frustration and not lash out at his wife and kids. This short-term suppression may work a few times, but very soon it will be depleted and the frustrated tirade will flow without control.

Willpower operates like sleep. You only have so many units of energy per day and it starts over each day when you wake up. Taking a nap in fact will recharge your body and your willpower. Other tools such as meditation, deep breathing, exercise, eating healthy and cold showers are all factors in how much willpower you have daily.

Willpower can be a great resource, especially in short-term situations, yet if you want to create lasting change, you will need more than a New Year's resolution and an hour of meditation per day. Doing the deep emotional work to pull out your bullets is the best way to make the kind of lasting long-term change that will cause 100lb of weight loss or rebuild the trust of your wife after decades of you being an asshole.

When a man first gets the slap, he is likely to go find a therapist to work with, start implementing changes and control his crappy communication habits for about four to eight weeks. It is around eight weeks that most temporary changes fall away, the willpower wears out, and the old habits come right back. At that point, your wife will put a finger in your face and say things like, "I knew it! I knew you wouldn't change. You'll never change." And she is right. If the only tool you employ, like most men, is your willpower, then nothing will change long-term and your marriage is doomed. Also, each time you watch your willpower fail you, your self-trust and confidence will take a hit.

My challenge to you is this: acknowledge and appreciate your willpower, but don't rely on it – it will wear out and fail you. Throw yourself headlong into the deep emotional work and make a new habit of turning to your tribe of men, venting out your feelings responsibly and celebrating your wins daily.

17
ARE YOU SO NEEDY THAT YOU REQUIRE YOUR WIFE TO RESPECT YOU?

One of the most common complaints we hear from men when they join The Bulletproof Husband is "She doesn't respect me." In response, we ask men to consider: "What kind of man *needs* his wife to respect him?"

If you *need* your wife to respect you, it means you are lacking the self-respect needed to fill your own cup. You are not complete and whole within yourself; you are acting from a place of being dependent on others, likely being clingy and needy. Women do not feel emotionally safe being married to a man who is not solid, complete and whole within himself.

When you are keeping your word to others and to yourself, you are operating within integrity and when you are consistent you will build trust with yourself. That feeling of integrity and trust within you creates respect toward yourself. In the same way that you would respect any other man who is consistent, reliable, integrous and trustworthy with his word, you will respect yourself when you are operating from that same place. Over time, other men will also begin to respect you as a man who is solid, consistent and reliable in his word.

When you gain respect from other men, you will observe that it has a different flavor to respect from your wife. Also, men typically seek out men they respect for having a specific expertise. So developing your strengths will also bring more masculine respect into your life.

It is best to have a hierarchy for respect: first, build respect for yourself, then gain the respect of other men, then last, gain your wife's respect as an optional bonus win.

While respect feels wonderful, the respect you get from your woman is best as a want, and not a need. I *want* my wife's respect. I *enjoy* her respect. It is the icing on the cake. But I don't *need* my wife's respect. If she isn't being respectful, it makes no difference to my inner world.

When I sense a loss of respect for me, I first check in with myself: "Have I done something to lose her respect?" Perhaps I have made a promise and didn't keep my word. In that case, I need to clean that up *so I can restore integrity with myself.* Start by being responsible for the current state of the low respect level. Second, recognize that there could be a million reasons why she isn't being respectful (she didn't sleep last night, she's having her period, she is going through menopause, a girlfriend was mean to her online, she ate some weird cheese, who the heck knows). When someone else is disrespectful, it's not personal, so if you are taking it personally, it means your bullets are engaged, and that's the problem you should be dealing with first and foremost.

SECTION RECAP

- Masculine dynamics: Macho/insecure is not masculine. Masculine/feminine creates polarity: masculine acts and then feels, feminine feels and then acts.
- Seven aspects: Know what you want, what you won't compromise on, ambitiously pursue, know your strengths and weaknesses, doesn't complain, is decisive and direct, simple and easy-going.
- Managing your confidence: There are three short-term and five long-term ways to raise your confidence.
- Tribe: You absolutely must build a masculine tribe of men that will challenge you and keep you accountable.
- Accountability: The ability to set an unwavering standard.
- Integrity: Your relationship in regard to your unwavering standard.
- 100% responsible: Your role of leading your marriage and family is based on never being a victim and on taking full ownership of everything around you.
- Willpower: This is a finite resource. It can be incredibly helpful, but also detrimental if it is your only tool.
- Self-respect: When you respect yourself and build your strengths, you will likely gain the overflow of other men and even your wife respecting you.

MEMBER STORY: FROM FRAGILE NICE GUY TO SOLIDLY MASCULINE

My whole life I was plagued by deep insecurities. I always felt inferior, like a separate category of a man, one that wasn't truly legitimate and that didn't deserve the kinds of relationships most people have. I had always thought I'd outgrow these insecurities, but by the time I reached my 40s, they only seemed to be getting worse, wreaking havoc on my happiness, marriage and almost every aspect of my life.

There came a point when I knew I had to take some action and address this. I had been in and out of counseling for years, which helped in some respects but never got to the core of my issues – my deep-rooted feelings of inadequacy. I prayed for guidance and became convinced that The Bulletproof Husband had the tools to help transform me into the confident and secure man I'd always wanted to become.

I immediately learned about pulling bullets, terms, purpose, and how to communicate with my wife. I realized all I had been doing wrong, and most importantly, I did some deep emotional work on myself. As I pulled several bullets and followed the program to the letter, my confidence slowly started to build. I started to become the consistent, reliable, stable man I'd always wanted to become. The sulking and pouting were eventually replaced with rock-solid confidence.

I remember a time at work when a direct report was disrespectful and out of line. Historically, I would have let it slide and changed the topic. This time, I called the colleague responsible out directly and with strength, in a way that he could not misunderstand or deny. His behavior changed from that time on, and I still take pride in how I was able to deal with this man in a masculine way.

I also saw clear changes in my relationship with my wife. I finally have her respect and am able to show up for her whenever she needs me. I can finally be her rock and her safe place, and our relationship has skyrocketed!

TBH gave me the exact tools that I needed to help transform me into the powerful, kind, secure man I've always wanted to be, and I've never been happier.

HOW TO MAKE MASCULINE DECISIONS

18
FIRST PRIORITY: KNOW YOUR TERMS

How do you know you are a man? Do you feel like a man simply because you have the biological parts? Do you tell yourself that you are a man because you do manly things like hiking, hunting, fishing, driving a big truck, fighting at the drop of a hat or putting another notch on your belt of sexual conquests?

While all those things can give you a rush of adrenalin and get your testosterone pumping, they are external and temporary answers to the question. For a man to feel solid in his masculinity, there must be an internal and unshakeable knowing of himself as a man. That internal core is what we call his "terms."

Whether you are 13 or 83 years old, your terms are core to who you are. When a man identifies and clarifies his terms, he knows what he would die for. A man's terms come before anything else in his life. For the vast majority of men, protecting their children from physical harm is a core part of their terms. This means that if a man must go off to war or protect his home from a burglar and give his life in the process, he will do so without hesitation because that is a core part of his terms as a man. If your child is running across the street and a bus is about to run them over, you would jump in front of the bus to save them and willingly get run over in the process, because like most men, protecting your child is a term for you. All men have terms – even if they haven't discovered them yet, they are buried within and you will benefit greatly if they are uncovered.

Once you are clear on your terms, you will be able to phrase them in simple statements that begin with "I am a man who..." Most men find that they have one to three terms that can be easily memorized. For example, my term is, "I am a man who provides safety and love for my family." There is a lot packed into that simple term. A man who *provides safety and love* speaks of a man who provides emotionally, financially, physically, mentally and spiritually for his family.

Take note that terms typically include the word "family" because it encompasses you as a member of your family. Many men fall into the trap of putting their own needs last because they are trying to serve their wife and children, while not knowing their terms. Often this leads to a man feeling like an emasculated "nice guy" who is actually very bitter and resentful inside because he has never valued his own needs. Knowing your terms and standing by them will make sure that your needs in life are taken care of. Outside of terms, you can allow life to happen around you, and as a bulletproof man, your terms are the only thing that you will control.

Common areas for terms are protecting and providing for one's family, being a man of faith and taking physical care of one's own fitness. Terms for these could look like this:

- I am a man who... stands firm in his faith.
- I am a man who... provides safety and love for his family.
- I am a man who... maintains his health diligently.

Figuring out your terms involves some trial and error. At first it is best to write out a few samples and carry them around in your pocket, reviewing them several times a day and refining them until they really feel representative of the most important aspects of who you are. The things that you will absolutely not compromise on. The things that you would be willing to get divorced or die over. An absurd example I like to use is if your wife said, "I'm tired of having three kids, let's drop them off at the forest and move to another country..." Your term of protecting your family would dictate that you drop your wife off at a mental asylum and protect your children from her. Your terms come before the marriage.

An important point is that your terms should never govern the acts of someone else – only you can act according to your terms. A lot of men try to come up with terms that control the actions of others, such as, "I am a man who won't be cheated on..." But that's not a term – that is really just hurt and insecurity coming to the surface to try to control your wife. Terms are about you and your actions, and *only you can violate your terms*.

In summary, once you have your terms figured out, your needs will be taken care of and your priorities will be clear. All feelings of emasculation will disappear from your life because as long as you are not violating your terms, you will feel rock solid and in touch with your masculine core.

Much more will be said about terms throughout this book, but for now, start by writing out your first few attempts at terms and begin refining them.

Warning: I cannot overstate how absolutely vital it is to know your terms. They should be so simple and clear that you could have them tattooed on your arm. The Bulletproof Husband program coaches are available to help members get clear on their terms. Don't half-ass this and try to go at it alone – get help.

19
SECOND PRIORITY: LET HER MANAGE THE RELATIONSHIP

When it comes to making decisions, there are clear filters that you can put your choices through. The first filter is your terms. If you won't be violating your terms by doing such and such, then your decision can pass to the second filter. The second filter is *cooperating with her management of the relationship.* The foundation of this concept is that women typically have a much higher skillset for interpersonal relationships. Imagine a triangle where she is at one corner, you are at one corner, and at the third corner is an entity known as "the relationship." She is the one who understands and cares for the needs of the relationship. While endless books and seminars have tried to train men to care for the needs of "the relationship," we continue to fail miserably. A better plan would be that we actually trust our wives and cooperate with their management of the relationship. Let them guide us regarding what the relationship needs. Instead of trying to figure out what the relationship needs, if we could simply live solidly within our terms, be the bowl for her feminine emotions and let her manage the relationship, she would be able to tell us exactly what the relationship needs moment by moment.

- But she is ignoring me and only stares at her damn phone all day!
- She is more interested in spending time with her girl-friends than me.
- She just uses me as a dumping ground for all her toxic emotions.
- She just bitches and complains to me about her mom and co-workers.
- She just uses me to do all the work around here.

These and many similar complaints are common among men. If we took a step back and actually trusted our wives to manage the relationship, we could simply be solid on our terms, be the bowl for her emotions and let her vent. When she is ignoring you, it is because she knows that is what the relationship needs in that moment. When she is more interested in spending time with her girlfriends, she knows that is what the relationship needs in that moment. When she is dumping all her messy emotions on you, trust that that is what the relationship needs in that moment.

Our pop culture has been trying to train men to manage the rela-tionship for a few decades, and men have felt pressured to make the relationship feel close and connected. Yet the paradigm I am describ-ing to you only obligates you to be solid in your terms and be the bowl for her emotions – beyond that, let her guide and manage the closeness or distance within the relationship.

Perhaps when she is ignoring you, she is actually testing to see if you are going to be clingy and needy. Or when she goes out to hang with her girlfriends, she is poking at you to see if you are going to get jealous. To the embittered man, these are stupid games that women play to torment us, yet to the bulletproof man, the nature of the feminine is constantly testing and challenging us to be more solid, while poking at our insecurities. Perhaps she doesn't see you as a dumping ground but as a trustable ear for her pain. Last, she isn't using you just to get things done around the house – she is giving you opportunities to show up and contribute to what matters to her.

The idea of trusting her management of the relationship may seem foreign to most men, yet this simple shift is massive. I was explaining the concept to a friend one day and she said, "Oh, that's just like Princess Buttercup and Prince Wesley in 'The Princess Bride' movie." Although that was a favorite from my childhood, I didn't understand what she was getting at, so I asked her to explain. "Well, at the beginning of the movie, Princess Buttercup has a servant boy named Wesley and she is always mean to him. She is constantly ordering him around and being bossy. Every time she barks an order at him, he says, 'As you wish.' After many years of this, Buttercup realized that when Wesley said, 'As you wish,' he was actually saying, 'I love you.' So when Wesley cooperated with her management of the relationship, she felt trusted and loved."

Yes! That is a great picture of what it means to cooperate with her management of the relationship. If her request doesn't cause you to violate a term, then regarding the relationship, the answer is: "As you wish."

20
THIRD PRIORITY: YOUR MASCULINE PURPOSE

From the ancients to today, men have always found great reward in purposeful action. The masculine innately responds to the drive of accomplishing a great goal or task, or even just chipping away at a great task daily. For most men, this is the area that builds their confidence the most. Going out to the office and accomplishing 12 things on your to-do list is a great confidence boost.

When a man gets the slap from his wife, often their *purpose realm* has been out of whack for a while. Perhaps he is like most men: he doesn't know his terms, he doesn't let her manage the relationship and he has made his purposeful work the top priority above his marriage and family. Alternatively, maybe he has made his family his purpose in life, so now he has been rocked by the slap and cannot gain confidence from his purpose because it is enmeshed with his family.

A man needs to have a purpose separate from his family and

marriage, and it needs to be a place he can go to emotionally where he can boost his confidence. He can then bring that boosted confidence back into his home and make a difference in his relationships. Most importantly, a man must know that his purpose comes third in the decision-making hierarchy.

Remember: terms come first, then letting her manage, and third is acting on your purpose. If your wife says that you two need a romantic weekend away, and that doesn't violate a term for you (such as you having given your word to a prior commitment, so going away would violate your integrity), then you should follow her management of the relationship and make it happen. Even if you want to do some purposeful work, you will need to put that on the backburner for now because it is a lower priority than cooperating with her management of the relationship.

Once you recognize the need for purpose in your life and grasp that it belongs as the third priority in how you make decisions, the final challenge you may face is finding a purpose to pour yourself into. One of the main differences between the masculine and the feminine is that the masculine acts and then feels, whereas the feminine feels and then acts. So, regarding purpose, don't get stuck in your head trying to find the perfect purpose. Just find something and take action. Then, you will feel the purposeful work fill you with feelings of accomplishment and confidence. Here's a thought exercise that can help you get started: *If you had a magic button to fix anything in the world, what would you fix? How can you take action today toward that end?*

21
FOURTH PRIORITY: YOUR FEELINGS AND WANTS

You have arrived at the fourth priority in the hierarchy of masculine decision-making. If your feelings are driving you to do something and it doesn't violate your terms, it doesn't conflict with her management of the relationship and it doesn't take away from you accomplishing your purpose, then you are in the realm of feelings and wants and you are free to do as you wish.

This may seem complicated, so let's consider an example. Your buddy asks you to go out for a drink on Friday night. This doesn't violate a term for you in any way, so you consider her management of the relationship: "Hey babe, my buddy wants to go out this Friday for a drink. Does this Friday work or what night would work for you?" This gives her the space to manage without giving her the control of only saying yes or no – instead, she has options to manage. Let's say she says, "Yes, Friday works; go for it." Then you check with yourself about your purpose, and whether going out for a drink with your buddy will make a significant difference to your purpose, which it won't, so you are good to go.

The interaction I just described should happen in a moment – it isn't some long, complicated process. Once ingrained, this four-step structure can easily guide all your decisions and keep you solid in your masculinity.

Without this structure, many men get themselves into hot water by not knowing their terms and constantly violating them, plus they don't cooperate with her management of the relationship – instead, they feel controlled by her and constantly try to please her and meet her needs so that they can get what they want (this is totally manipulative). Lastly a lot of men don't acknowledge that terms meet their needs, but not their feelings and wants, which are the fourth priority and come at the bottom of the list. A solid man doesn't let his feelings and wants to run his life; that is a bullet-driven, sloppy and unmasculine way to live your life.

If you put your feelings and wants above your purpose, her management, or, God forbid, your terms, then you are living your life driven by your emotions. You are doing what the scariest men do: you are living as the water and not as the bowl. Your wife will have to tip-toe around on eggshells because she doesn't want to trigger you. Bottom line, your wife will have to baby-sit your feelings, which repels any healthy feminine romantic relationship she can offer and pushes away healthy masculine friendships your friends can offer.

Warning: It is vital to know the difference between having emotions versus being emotional. All men have emotions, even if you pull all your bullets, you will still be a human being and one of the best parts of life are the emotions you get to experience. Have your emotions and be responsible for them. The only emotion that we recommend you don't show around your wife and kids is anger and the cousins of anger (frustration, irritation, annoyance, etc). Having emotions is vastly different than "Being emotional." Being emotional means that you are lead by your emotions, you make your choices from your emotions.

You are not living your life in the proper masculine frame of Terms/Management/Purpose/Feelings; instead you are allowing your feelings to take the top place. When you do that, you are going to turn your life into a dumpster fire of constant reactions and explosions. Have emotions, experience them fully, but don't be emotional and never let them guide your decisions.

SECTION RECAP

- Knowing your terms: Your terms are the very essence of your authentic masculine core. If you compromise your terms, you are not being you. They come before anything else in all your relationships.
- Cooperating with her management of the relationship: Her skillset of managing relationships is far superior to yours; when you try to manage, it typically will feel controlling to her.
- Being purposeful: You need a purpose outside of your family. This is a place that you can go to build your confidence and then bring that confidence back to your relationship.
- Your wants and feelings: After you have fulfilled your obligations to the previous three priorities (terms, her management, your purpose), you are free to do as you want and feel.

MEMBER STORY: FROM ROCK BOTTOM REACTIONS TO POWERFUL RESPONSES AND RESTORATION

It was a quiet Sunday morning. My one-year-old son was in the living room with my wife on the couch. My dad had just stopped over to give us payment for the new backdoor we had installed and to see how things were going. I still remember the look of concern on his face when he said, "She doesn't look good; make sure you take care of her." He was referring to my wife, who had been dealing with two minor health issues over the summer. A conversation of her health turned into raised voices, we started to yell, and then I did it. I grabbed her and my son from the couch, with a firm grasp of my hands around my wife's frail biceps. I took my son into the adjacent room, and continued to converse with my wife. I then left with my son to go to my dad's, so she could rest.

Ten months later: "Do it to me," my friend said to me.

"Do what?" I asked.

"Grab me off the couch, just like you did your wife," my friend said.

"Why what's it going to prove?" I questioned.

She said, "Just do it."

With all the trust in my heart, I pulled my friend from the couch like I had done that day that broke my marriage. As my fingers left my friends arm, I could remember the way my fingers felt only bone in my wife's arms, and how it compared to my friend's arms just then. I sat down, in disappointment. My friend said, "I just can't imagine you doing it."

As I left my friend's house, I just restated their "I just can't imagine you doing it." I couldn't either. How had I let all my past pains and emotions get the best of me? How could I have let it get so bad that I lost control of myself, and created a space of fear, doubt, pain, and distance between myself, and the family I had just created? How could I physically touch her that way, and then physically lose the business we had built, the house we'd remodeled, and the dreams we'd started to build?

My wife had to create a safe place for herself, and our relationship to heal. We didn't directly interact for seven months because she felt it necessary to have restraining order, and had also pressed charges for domestic assault.

I had to do the emotional work to never be that man again, and never put my son in a place that wasn't safe for him or my wife. It was then I realized that from the work I had been doing, my friend not only couldn't see the man I had been in the past, but would also only ever know the new man I'd started to become.

Seventeen months after that event, which had been the final straw for my wife, we are back together. We live under one roof in a committed relationship, even after we divorced.

I'm rebuilding my family, my dreams, and my business in a healthy balance of the things that matter most to me in life. I have an amazing, vocal, expressive, funny, three-year-old – someone I wouldn't have been able to give up seeing for the rest of my life on a Christmas morning opening presents from Santa.

My wife and I have a relationship where we talk through the complex situations of life, we talk about our feelings and we face life as a team. It wasn't easy to get here. It was a lot of commitment, it took a lot of sacrifices, changes in both our lives, and long hours of talking to, listening to and learning from each other.

As of November 6, 2021, we are officially remarried. We continue to grow as a couple, and the work never ends. That was one piece of the past relationship that we both failed to realize – that in this life, our relationship is a continuous journey.

UNDERSTANDING YOUR JOURNEY

22
YOU ARE DANGLING FROM A CLIFF – NOW WHAT?

Imagine that you are hanging from your fingertips on the side of a cliff with your heart racing... What does this picture mean to you? Are you about to slip and fall to a terrifying death or are you a professional rock climber having the time of your life! The difference between these two perspectives is called "context." You are always the one who determines your context, your interpretation, the meaning or filter that you are going to use to understand the world around you.

When you experience a sudden shocking event, such as receiving the slap from your wife, you can see that as the death of your marriage (which is one context), or you can see it as a new beginning where you rebuild yourself into the man she would be a fool to leave (another context). Neither context is right or wrong, but each context bears its own fruit.

In life, you always get to choose your context. You can choose one that makes you a victim (e.g. "Why do bad things always happen to me?"), or you can choose an empowering context (e.g. "God or the universe is always conspiring in my favor and giving me opportunities to grow!"). This may seem a bit naive, yet even the famed psychologist Viktor Frankl noted in his book "Man's Search for Meaning," which recounts life in the Nazi concentration camps of WWII, that "Between stimulus and response there is a space. In that space is our power to choose our response. In our response lie our growth and our freedom." If this wisdom is usable and observable within a concentration camp, then surely it can be applied in any situation.

The idea of choosing your context is fundamental to being bulletproof. No matter what life throws at you, you can choose the most empowering context and reframe the situation to work for your benefit. The bulletproof man can see a heart attack as a wakeup call that will push him to a new level of health. A bankruptcy can be an opportunity for a fresh start but with all the lessons from the past, so as not to make the same mistakes. The slap from your wife could be the breaking point that brings you to the edge of hopelessness and despair, or it could be the inspiration to become the man you've always wanted to be, the man she'd be a fool to leave.

How are you seeing the situations in front of you right now? Perhaps your marriage is in shambles, your health is declining, your children are emotionally devastated, your work is shaky and your confidence is a wreck. Yet in each of these areas, you can choose a different perspective. You can give yourself the gift of a powerful context.

My friend and mentor, Dr. Gary Menezes, frequently uses a coffee cup on his desk as a metaphor for understanding context. He asks the question, "Why is this coffee cup on my desk? Well, it could be because it was the only clean one in the cupboard this morning, so it's the one I chose. Or it could be because my wife got it as a gift for our anniversary 10 years ago and it's my favorite. It could be because I am too lazy to go put it in the sink. It could be because someone invented the coffee cup hundreds of years ago because they were driven to impress others with their brilliant invention. All of these answers could simultaneously be true and I could make up a billion more reasons to answer the question 'Why is the coffee cup on my desk?'. At the end of the day, though, I am simply picking one of the billion reasons. The same is true of how we interpret everything in life. When someone asks, 'Why is this happening?', the answer they give themselves is simply their brain picking one of the billion reasons; with that being the case, choose the most empowering reason that you can give yourself, even if it sounds like bullshit. 'Why is my wife asking for a separation?' It could be because you're an asshole and she hates you, or it could be because she wants space to heal and to give you a chance to work on yourself so that you can build a better future together. The bottom line is: you get to give yourself the gift of an empowering context."

One of my favorite contexts is from the former Navy Seal Commander Jocko Willink. No matter what life or war threw at him, his context was a steely-eyed look on his face and uttering the word: "Good." He would get something good out of anything that was happening. Do yourself a favor and take on the same self-empowering mentality.

23
WHY IS SHE BEING SUCH A B*TCH?

She wakes up one morning and stumbles down the stairs to the kitchen where you are cooking eggs for the family. She takes one look at the pan and says, "Ugh, eggs again. You are so boring." She then slumps into a chair with her coffee mug and stares into her phone for the next 30 minutes. Once the kids have headed out the door to school, she gets herself dressed, and snaps at you that your shirt is ugly and that you need to lose weight. Finally, as she gets in her car, she yells at you out the window that you forgot to refill her gas and she is going to be late to work because you are such a lazy ass.

At this point, it is super-easy to drop into victim mode and get bitter about how you are being treated. You could also go into judgment mode and think about putting up boundaries regarding her "disrespect and bitchiness." Yet let's jump back to the previous chapter about context for a minute. Here's where the rubber meets the road.

Is she being bitchy or is she testing you? Is she being disrespectful or is she poking you to check for your bullets? Is she being mean or is she trying to see if you have become an emotionally solid bowl that can handle her splashing? What if you actually took on the context that everything she did – literally EVERYTHING she did – was a test. Constantly, without reservation, the feminine is always testing the masculine for emotional solidness, safeness and presence.

Are you going to dwell on your *Victim bullet*, your *Loser bullet* and your *Stupid bullet*, or are you going to dwell on a solid context, see her feminine splashing as simply a test, and pass that test? You can decide to see it all as a test, where each time she pokes at you, she is doing you a favor. Use the exit strategy if you need to. Go for a quick scream in your car, privately yell everything you would want to scream in her face, and get it all out, then get back to the house and keep passing those tests.

Warning: When her splashing bothers you, you have to do the emotional work of pulling out the bullet she is poking. Otherwise, you are not moving forward into becoming a better man; you are simply suffering and suppressing more hurt, and eventually your willpower will give out and you will explode at her. Be responsible and do the emotional work.

24
DON'T FORGET TO STACK UP YOUR GAINS

To be a solid man, you need to take responsibility for managing your own confidence, and one of the fastest and most practical ways to boost your confidence is to track your wins.

A "win" is a context that you can choose. There are both internal and external wins. Most men are more familiar with external wins, so we will start with understanding those.

When you get a financial raise at work, when you lose 10lb of fat, when your wife compliments you about something you accomplished, these boost your confidence. You feel good about yourself and emotionally stronger to take on greater challenges. These are wins that you have gained externally. External wins are great, but they are outside your control. Your boss might not like you for some reason and pass you over for the raise, you might have some inflammation and register higher on the scale, your wife might be in a foul mood and criticize you, and just like that, poof! Your confidence is gone and you feel flat and deflated.

That is why internal wins are even more important and stabilizing. An internal win comes from recognizing how you are showing up in your life as the man you've always wanted to be. A clear example would be how a paramedic could recognize his internal wins. Let's say he shows up on the scene of a car accident. There are bad injuries and is it a very stressful and distressing situation. This situation presents no external wins – there is nothing good about a car accident itself. Yet he is able to treat the injuries, bring calm and safety to the very scared individuals and bring comfort to the bystanders. At the end of the day, he can look back at how he brought peace, calm, safety and comfort to those people. He can pat himself on the back for being the kind of man that brings wonderful things to terrible situations.

Take some time each day to look back over the day and acknowledge your external wins, even the small ones: I washed the dishes. I worked out. I fed my kids a good dinner. I helped them with homework. I filled out my TPS report at work[9]. I was solid when my wife was testing me by being mean about my weight. Then, dig deeper to find the internal wins: I am becoming the kind of man who values his health by exercising and eating well. I am being a great father by showing up for my kids with their homework. I am proud of myself for dealing with my Loser bullet and being more solid when she was poking fun at my weight.

When you track your wins daily, even simply having a habit of recognizing three external and three internal wins at the end of your day, you are taking responsibility for your confidence level and proactively growing your confidence to the next level. This will cause you to be triggered less often and to be more solid in every situation.

The power of tracking your wins cannot be overstated. It is best to keep a daily "wins journal" and review it whenever you need to boost your confidence.

9| Yes, this is a reference to the movie "Office Space." You're welcome.

25
FROM ZERO TO HERO

A powerful context that I found while going through my marital separation and publicly humiliating myself by destroying my reputation and marriage is what's known as The Hero's Journey. As far as contexts go, it is a powerful one to hold onto when you are on a deep growth journey.

Whether it is Harry Potter, Luke Skywalker, or Frodo Baggins, the hero's journey is the same. Joseph Campbell was a famous anthropologist who researched native stories from all around the world and found that throughout history, we have all been telling the same story over and over again. The tale is actually the journey that we all walk many times in our lives as we go through phases of growth.

Essentially there are 12 points on the circular journey of growth that the hero walks. He begins in the (1) ordinary world such as Tatooine or the Shire, where he receives the (2) call to adventure such as the invitation to Hogwarts, which is commonly followed by the (3) refusal of the call. Many times the hero tries to stay in their comfort zone. This refusal is followed by (4) meeting a mentor such as Gandalf, Obi-wan Kenobi, or Dumbledore. After meeting the mentor, the hero leaves the ordinary world and descends into the (5) special world, into the darkness, or as Carl Jung called it, the unconscious. Once in the special world, the hero has left the ordinary world far behind and must face (6) tests, enemies and dragons. Typically he will also make some allies and friends for the rest of the journey. After a measure of success, the hero must (7) approach the innermost cave, such as when Luke Skywalker had to face his fear of Darth Vader in the cave on Dagobah. This leads to the hero's (8) greatest ordeal, which often deeply transforms the hero into an upgraded version of himself. The successful ordeal gives the hero a (9) new power. It may be a magical power, potion, a special sword, or even the love of his special woman – regardless, something is given to the hero, and he has earned it. Once the hero has been upgraded, he realizes that he must (10) journey back to the ordinary world, but he isn't out of the woods yet. He still will face his greatest challenge one last time, and in that last battle, the hero will muster all the lessons and special gifts and skills gained from the special world. Once he defeats his enemy, he is permanently a new man – this stage of struggle is referred to as (11) resurrection. Finally, the hero (12) returns to the ordinary world – the Shire, or, as the last movie in the "Skywalker Saga" ends, with Rey back on Tatooine where young farmer Luke began.

In returning, the hero always brings back the reward that they gained from the ordeal in step 7. This can be insight, wisdom, superpowers or a magic elixir that will heal others. The upgraded version of the hero then lives among the ordinary world and is a help to others. Often this journey includes narcissists going on a journey from being selfish at step 1 to being self-giving by step 12, such as the journey of the self-absorbed Iron Man in the "Avengers" series, who ultimately sacrifices himself to save his friends.

I was able to use the context of these 12 steps as a compass in the darkness. I'll give you a brief overview. My ordinary world was serving in full-time ministry as a public speaker and being in a marriage of 14 years. My call to adventure was the public failure and collapse of my international ministry, which led to a separation from my wife. Struggling with all my might, I tried to refuse the call to adventure and didn't want to leave my ordinary world. Then a mentor came along and gave me hope that he could guide me through the special world, and I capitulated and crossed the threshold. I faced tests and challenges by getting psychologists and counselors to help me address my inner demons. I also made new friends and allies during this phase of my journey.

Then, I faced the ordeal and thought I had gained some new potion and began my journey back to the Shire. Little did I know that when I was confronted again at the resurrection stage, I would fail. I failed because I hadn't actually dealt with issues in the innermost cave back in step 7, this led to a second round of publicly humiliating myself and a second (deeper) separation from my wife.

After two years, I was starting back at step 4, with a new mentor (The Bulletproof Husband program), crossing the threshold again into the special world and facing my dragons without many of those who had journeyed with me the first time. The second cycle moved much more quickly and I was able to properly slay the dragons this time because of my new insights. Within months, I was at step 10 on the road back to the Shire. Our marriage was reunited and those still walking with me were able to see the transformation. At that point, I arrived at the resurrection stage and spoke to the public once again for the first time in two and a half years. I spoke the truth without mincing words. I owned my actions and took responsibility for the lies I had believed, which had led me to my previous behaviors. Now back in the ordinary world as an upgraded version of myself, I am thankful for the journey I have been on and I share the elixir that I gained.

So where are you in your hero's journey? What mentor is guiding you through the special world? Who is your new tribe of allies that will journey with you? What must you face in the innermost cave? Have you gained the elixir? Are you sharing your elixir with others?

SECTION RECAP

- Choose your context: You are always interpreting everything that is happening in your life. You get to choose what anything and everything mean.
- She is testing you: A powerful context you can use is to see all her behavior as a test for you as a man. This will keep resentment away from you by keeping you from taking things personally.
- Own your wins: Once you see that you can reframe the meaning of everything in your life, you can then begin to find wins in anything, which will boost your confidence.
- The hero's journey: All cultures over all times have essentially told the same story, it is a 12-part story of how the hero grows through challenges. You are the hero in your own life journey and you can use this 12-part framework to understand exactly where you are in your process.

MEMBER STORY: FROM LOSERVILLE TO WIN CITY!

The lights in Vegas shine bright. So bright that you can even see them in space. They need no explanation. Loud music and lights in Vegas mean lots of fun and excitement. Everyone wants to win. Win small or win BIG, it is about the rush we get when it hits JACK-POT or the dealer turns your cards to reveal a blackjack! You see, Vegas and the "Win City" have a LOT in common. I live in Win City. It's not magic, but it is a place where you get to on days when you are winning!

Let me bring you back to a Saturday in the fall of 2018. I was standing outside. Children were laughing and playing. You could smell the fresh cut grass. Popcorn popping, burgers grilling, excitement and the smell of sweat filled the air. It was my first football game officiating as the head official. I was thrilled. I stood there, envisioning myself as a little kid thinking that one day, I would be on a field just like this. Blood was rushing through my veins as a calm came over me. This was what I had worked so hard for... The game flashed in an instant and was over. I was elated as a kid to share.

When I got home, I wasn't able to share. You see, my wife was there packing and leaving. Box by box and item by item, pieces of my home disappeared. Soon she would be gone. My years of neglecting my wife and everyone around me had taken a huge toll. It was then I realized I was not living and I had to do something to better who I was. It was the bottom. I knew I had to be better and responsible for my actions!

After a thorough ass-whopping and using the tools provided to me through The Bulletproof Husband program, I took accountability and started to live with responsibility. Emotional work became a part of my life. I would eat and sleep the emotional work and discovered a new passion to aid others in being better people.

Now, I am leading hundreds of games as an official. My daughter is launching three-pointers. I am truly living responsibility. The old me would have been complaining and a victim. The new me enjoys these moments with my daughter: I lead with a purpose and have a woman to whom I listen and own my responsibilities.

Days go by and as I own my responsibilities and actions, things light up. The wins pile up.

My ex-wife and I talk frequently. I have given her many bullet-proof apologies. When she was in town, we found time to hang out to enjoy each other's company. Over time, I met other ladies but truly kept being called back to an old friend.

In May 2021, I began developing a new relationship with an amazing woman. This woman would challenge me in every area I thought I was good. I would do work around every domain in my life. Each step enabled me to be the man I am today. In order to gain even more clarity, I took another step in the TBH program and went to the retreat. During the retreat, I was inspected around my plan to get married. This inspection showed me an area in which I was ashamed. Over the past few weeks, I have focused on implementing the changes in my life to be the man I want to be. The final hours of the retreat, my wins just rolled and the lights in my city were on high beams!

I continue daily to boost my confidence and coach other men to be the men they want to be. Every day, I encounter new bullets or a bullet coming from a new direction. If I react, I do the work and complete the process. No matter whether it's work, family, finances, or even the lady who I plan one day to get engaged to and marry, my life lights up like Win City! Trust the process. Do the work, see the results! (Light up your Win CITY!)

DEAL WITH YOUR BULLETS

26
YOUR INSECURITY IS RELATIONAL PESTICIDE

A bullet is a metaphor to describe emotional wounds. Say, for example, that a little boy is regularly beaten and then tells himself that this is happening because he is "weak." That boy will grow up thinking he is weak and needs to overcompensate by becoming powerful, which will lead him to be controlling and manipulative. This is referred to as a *Weak bullet*. When that man gets married, his wife will figure out within a few months that he has a Weak bullet lodged in his chest and she will poke at it to wake him up to deal with it. This typically leads to the man reacting to the pain of having his bullet-hole poked and becoming triggered, defensive, exploding externally or imploding internally, and going to find something to numb the pain of the bullet. This cycle of her poking, him being triggered, him numbing the pain, and then trying harder to overcompensate for the bullet, is the bullet cycle that I was stuck in for three decades and many men are stuck in for their entire lives.

Most of our deep bullets are put there in childhood. When something painful happens in a child's life, they try to figure out why and the answer they arrive at typically involves blaming themselves with a label: *because I am stupid, evil, weak, a loser, etc.* These labels are not just mental; they are emotional bullet wounds that we self-inflict. The events of our childhood were simply events that happened, they are facts from long ago, yet what lingers with us is the bullets we have given to ourselves. Nobody ever gives someone else a bullet. Bullets are self-inflicted.

As grown men, emotional bullet wounds are what account for all our insecurities, self-hatred, arguing, defending, boasting, debating, addictions, pleasing and approval-seeking behaviors. If you didn't have bullets, you wouldn't be driven to these behaviors. All of us are living in reaction to bullet-holes we gave ourselves, likely decades ago.

27
WHAT'S UP, SHORTY?

There's a classic scene in the 2003 Christmas comedy "Elf" where Will Ferrell's clueless elf character enters a board meeting and mistakes Peter Dinklage, who stands at 4'5", for a fellow elf. He really digs into Peter's insecurity about his height by asking, "Does Santa know that you left the workshop? Did you have to borrow a reindeer to get down here?"

Peter's bullets get triggered and he responds with, "Hey jack-weed, I get more action in a week than you have gotten in your entire life. I have houses in LA, Paris and Vail, each one of them with a 70" plasma screen, so I suggest you wipe that stupid smile off your face before I come over there and smack it off."

Will's character can't help himself and responds to those around the board meeting, "He's an angry elf." Which then leads to Peter running down the boardroom table and doing a flying double-kick to Will's chest, followed by an armbar throw onto the table.

We can all understand this scene because it is exactly how we feel when our insecurities are being poked. If Peter's character wasn't insecure about his height, he wouldn't have been triggered by Will's ridiculous comments. Like when you say to your really tall friend, "What's up, shorty?" It doesn't bother him because he isn't insecure about being short. So if your wife is able to trigger you, it is because of *your insecurity*. It is time to stop blaming her, defending yourself, getting triggered and arguing; it is time to take personal responsibility. If what your wife says or does triggers any emotionality in you, then there is a button inside of you that she is pushing and it is *your responsibility* to own that and deal with it. The potential here is that if you do the emotional work to pull out your bullets, nothing anyone else does will trigger you.

28
DO YOU EVEN LIFT, BRO?!

In the M. Night Shyamalan movie "Lady in the Water" (2006), there is a character who is constantly doing bicep curls with only one arm. By the time the character is introduced, he is absolutely laughable because of his one giant muscular arm. And this is similar to how bullets affect us as men. Imagine that a seven-year-old version of yourself picked up a gun and accidently shot yourself in the left arm and it never healed properly. Now, as an adult, you likely would have learned to overcompensate by avoiding using your left arm and constantly using your right arm. This is exactly what bullets do in us emotionally.

Let's say that you felt like you were behind in your schooling and your teachers didn't like interacting with you. A young version of yourself may have said, "It must be because I am stupid." That is how a person gives themselves the *Stupid bullet*. You then proceeded to read, study and get an advanced college degree to make up for the bullet deep inside which is telling you that you are actually stupid. Those with a Stupid bullet constantly argue, debate, use complicated and unusual vocabulary and lots of words to say things that could be stated clearly and directly. These symptoms are all common to men with a Stupid bullet.

On the flip side, the effect of a bullet is not all bad. When each bullet is overcompensated for, other muscles are developed. Such as the character from "The Lady in the Water," as his massive bicep came in very useful later in the movie. In the same way, the man with the Stupid bullet that drives him to study hard may end up writing many useful books, developing philosophies, or creating governmental structures that have never been seen. Each bullet has a positive and a negative. Once the bullet is actually removed, the negative side is gone, but the positive side remains. If a Stupid bullet is removed, the insecurities that used to drive the arguing, debating and the need to be right will be gone, but all the wisdom and knowledge that was gathered over the years will remain within the man.

Bullets create insecurity and turmoil in our relationships, yet they also produce incredible, positive accomplishments as well. Think of the kid who says, "I'm a loser," who then goes on to build a major business that provides employment for thousands of others, or the kid that says, "I am weak," who then goes on to train endlessly and win at the Olympics. There are many other examples I could give, and I challenge you to look at your own strengths and figure out some bullets that may have driven you to accomplish everything you have so far.

29
MAYBE YOU'RE A NARCISSIST, BUT LIKELY YOU'RE JUST AN ASSH*LE

Like most men, when your wife gave you the slap, it may have come with some "labels." You are "a narcissist," "emotionally abusive," "a sex addict," "a gaslighter," etc. This may be the result of getting input from her girlfriends, blogs, memes, online videos or even a psychiatrist. Our modern Western culture has become absolutely obsessed with "diagnosing" everyone with a label and getting them into some sort of endless treatment plan or medication.[10] My advice to you: don't go down that rabbit hole.

If you use the tools to ask your wife *open-ended questions* (OEQs) and make her feel *heard, understood, appreciated and valued* (HUAV), while consistently using 80/20 communication

10| "The Myth of Mental Illness" by Dr. Thomas Szasz.

and being a solid bowl, the labels will melt away as trust is rebuilt.

Many men are offended by the labels their wife uses, and the best thing to start with is giving yourself a label that is all-encompassing. At The Bulletproof Husband, we typically just use "asshole" as a catch-all. For example, she says to you, "You are such a narcissist; all you do is gaslight me and blame-shift. I am so sick of your emotionally abusive behavior." You can respond with, "I agree, I have been a huge asshole. Can you tell me how it has felt being married to me?" Then STFU and listen! It doesn't matter what labels she uses, what matters is that she gets it out and that she feels heard[11]. It is poison trapped in her and you are helping her heal by venting it out.

Don't get stuck on a pseudo-medical-sounding label that she or some therapist have slapped on you; just do the emotional work and use the tools, and own the "asshole" label when needed. Also, don't get triggered by the labels she throws at you. If it helps, then own them – it won't make a difference in the long run. "So you keep saying I am a narcissist, and I looked it up and it makes sense to me. I think I have a lot of those behaviors; can you tell me which ones you see the most in me?" Then STFU and listen!

11| David Deida's book "The Way of the Superior Man" has an excellent chapter on this idea entitled: "Her complaint is content free." Essentially, stop getting hung up on her words.

30
NINE DIFFERENT CALIBERS

In the previous chapters we saw how bullets are insecurities that we inflict on ourselves, and that when we experience life we label and blame ourselves. That is the definition of a bullet. We also saw that whenever there is an emotional reaction, there is a bullet in play. Also, bullets cause us to develop some of our greatest strengths as well as our insecurities. We also looked at three of the most common bullets, (1) Stupid, (2) Loser and (3) Weak. Here we will briefly cover six more of the nine most common bullets.

The (4) **Incompetent bullet** shows up when you feel overwhelmed and incapable of handling the circumstances around you. The incompetent bullet has shown up for me often in parenting my children. At those moments where my three young daughters are all crying and screaming, we are late for an appointment, or nobody will sleep through the night, those were the times I'd feel that bullet getting poked.

Throughout this chapter I will include a descriptive narrative with each bullet about an imaginary man named "Jack." Jack represents the thousands of men that we have seen with each of these bullets.

Jack's grandfather was a superhero, a great man. Served in the war, raised eight children, was a leader in the church, a cornerstone of the community. Harrowing tales of valor, triumphs, and aspirations filled little Jack's imagination. His father, however, was a divorced failed businessman, and placed all the family hopes and dreams on Jack to carry the "family name" and succeed where he had failed, to be "Just like his grandfather." The badge of honor soon became a heavy weight under such pressure to live up to the lofty standards.

With expectations so high, always out of reach, Jack sought approval for every accomplishment big or small to fit into the myth of his father's. "Your grandfather was 20 when stormed the beaches" was a common retort to Jack's complaints. Nothing Jack could do to get out of the shadow of his grandfather's legend, which was always 10 steps ahead, "This is meaningless!" he shouted at the stars.

To try to close the gap, Jack took short cuts on tests, taxes and love. He became a business fraud, and an annoyance to be around at dinner parties with his bragging and delusions of grandeur, promising his wife the world... always just one business deal away. Only in foreclosure did he look into the mirror of the lost man within. Who was he?

The "unrealized dream of his own" was the answer. What was his gift? His success? To him? Nobody ever asked... not even Jack. He was an automaton, punching in every day for someone else's dream, polishing a statue that wasn't his. All this time wasted in secret rebellion and regret for approval he never got, the incompetence an outward expression of this war within.

The (5) **Victim bullet** is the one that appears with the feeling that you are being abused or mistreated. It may be true that someone is hurting you, but the victim bullet will make you powerless and keep you there. It causes you to finger point, blame, and make excuses rather than being responsible and moving forward with your life regardless of what you have experienced.

Here we find Jack again:

Jack always ended up on the receiving end of the abuse his older brother dealt out. Overpowered, robbed of his power, Jack succumbed to his brother's strength, size and experience. Jack loved his brother when he was more like a brother, playing toy cars in the sand pit. However, out of seemingly nowhere, his brother would strike. Physically, the punches hurt, but the emotional daggers to his heart were the ones that never stopped bleeding. The pain of his brother's constant aggression and betrayals grew in Jack: "I will get his revenge" he plotted. Tacks put in his brothers pillowcase, spit in his soup, holes in his bike tire – there were many ways.

As the years wore on, others would take the place of his emotional back-stabber. Anyone was a candidate to rob his power from him: girlfriends, friends, work-mates, a stranger not turning quickly enough when the traffic light changed – "Move it, asshole!" Particularly those he would give his heart to in love. Those daggers lodged deep in his back; he would count nightly in the mirror.

"They're all out to get me," he swore under his breath. Even the slightest jest in his direction was a direct assault, to be met with a counter-assault or a dark thought. He joined organizations and cause after cause for those who were victims of injustice, while blaming his children and wife at the drop of a dime. Jack played the victim/victimizer in a never-ending cycle of passive aggressive blame, always justified... always! His divorce would drag out for years, based on this perspective of reality: no detail too small to fight in court, or him being purposefully late in dropping off the kids to match the time his ex was late. Through his victimhood, the ones who mattered most, his children, became the biggest victims of all.

The (6) **Broken bullet** tells you that you are not good enough, that you will never be good enough, you are not lovable, and why? Because you are broken! And because you think you are broken, you will need to prove that you are perfectly whole and complete, that you have no issues whatsoever. You will cover up your imperfections with perfectionism.

"Don't ever have children," "I never wanted children," and the dreaded "You were an accident," were often repeated quips by Jack's mother. Sometimes in humor, sometimes in frustration. Often enough for this little boy to begin to believe that he was the problem... all of the problems, the curse of his mother's existence. She shared her dream of traveling the world while independently running a salon, and how it all had all come to a crashing end when she had him.

"I am not meant to be," he often thought. His interests

were not her interests. His world overlooked diminished, invalidated by her narrative. His story was always pushed aside for her story, by her.

Boiling bubbling resentment grew in Jack's angst. Denying his own expression/thoughts/feelings became habitual "It doesn't matter. I'm fine. I'll get over it." Drinking and drugging it away made him further disassociate. Others' pain? They would just have to cope like him. Theirs could never match the pain he felt. He attracted women who "put him down" and other women who put up with him lashing out... for a time. In his dreams, Jack was a world-renowned daredevil, a rush of adrenaline coupled with dancing on the edge death: he soared down over the mountain face in his cliff diving suit.

Freedom and peace he found in testing his mortality, alive at last when dancing with death. But even this was only a temporary escape from the resentment he felt towards women and life. Depression was a specter that followed him through failed relationship after failed relationship. Nothing ever stayed together, and everything was, eventually, broken.

The (7) **Burden bullet** says that you are extra, unneeded, unwanted and will need to work your tail off to prove yourself valuable and worthwhile having around. Many people in ministry or humanitarian services are self-sacrificing because of being driven by the burden bullet. The inability to receive and the feelings of unworthiness are ever present.

Jack carried a heavy burden from childhood. He dragged himself through life, boulders crushing weight on his back, dragging a ship anchor behind him. Every word from his mouth was a weighted brick of disappointment. Jack's parents had abandoned him in their own personal dramas, and had never really paid much attention to him. He was an inconvenience, a second thought. They'd never really taken the time to love him the way he needed to be loved. "What can I do without their love?" he whimpered alone. Left with this feeling, he made it about himself, judging himself unworthy of their love, even unlovable. "Your authentic self will not be loved, so you have to be something else rather than accept this fate," he said in hopes of a savior. "I'll wear a mask, and become something they will love."

While being the recluse at home, being small, not inconveniencing others with his presence, apologizing for his existence, Jack learned to please his parents, trying on different performances: the "Hard Worker," the "Jester," the "Savior" of his parent's emotions, taking more of their burden off them. Slowly the authentic part of him disappeared – that was the unloved part after all – and the more he became the fake personas that gave him the attention he desired.

Enter the "Rock Star"! The die had been cast. Jack's fake love, attained by fake acting, would simply disappear into a bottomless, non-substantive hole in his heart. The feeling of appreciation had become his drug, boosting his depleted confidence in himself. When that was gone, he was gone. He moved on to bigger venues in search of all the attention he could possibly get: a love drug hit from the masses.

On stage, the adoring throngs lavished him with love and appreciation, overflowing the well in his heart, while he performed. Backstage... all alone... all that love disappeared and the drug wore off, so he would do a line of coke to try and wash away the new feeling of abandonment he was reliving. The panic set in after the well in his heart dried up. "Will they still love me?"

From the highest heights, to the crashing lowest of lows, fears and terrors of abandonment and loneliness of his childhood clawed their way back. "Someone will discover nobody loved me, it was all fake, I'm a fake." Unappreciated for who was under the makeup, Jack proceeded to trash his penthouse suite!

The (8) **Weird/Ugly/Different bullet** puts a voice in your head that says a lot of mean things to you about how you won't fit in and how others see you as something to look down on. You are the Quasimodo hunchback and need to try harder to fit in and be the same as everyone else.

Jack always thought of himself as the "black sheep," as if he were looking into the social bubble from the outside. He never felt like he belonged, even as a child. His mother constantly undermined him, manipulating him to do what she wanted, never loving him in the way he needed.

'Liar!' she called him, questioning his every intent, convincing him his intentions were always sinister. Over time he began to believe he was untrustworthy, not trusting his own thoughts. As he tried to figure out why he wasn't trusted by his mother, he felt his way down a logic chain to try to make sense of why he felt the way he did: "If my mother doesn't trust me, how can I trust myself? If I can't be trusted, then I can't be loved. If I can't be loved, I can't be trusted..." He took this all the way to the ultimate conclusion, "I can't trust love."

Later in life Jack tried to compensate for not trusting love. He constantly snooped on his wife, checking her phone, her social media, accusing her of things she wasn't doing (but he was sure she was). He had at the ready a list of ways he'd loved her, and the ways she didn't love him. In the end he became the manipulator, just like his mother. Because all his attempts to get the love from her (that he needed from his mother) didn't work in his relationship, he turned to the one feeling that made him feel love... sex. Sex in his mind made him feel loved and became the measurement of love in his relationship. So as she became more and more disinterested in sex, he became more and more resentful, blaming her for not loving him.

Jack's smothering and persistent anger at her for not giving him "what was due" widened the rift until she fell off the relationship, and ended up doing what he feared most. His self-fulfilling prophecy came true.

The (9) **Mean/Selfish/Evil bullet** torments your mind about how terrible a person you are. That you must try to look perfect because otherwise everyone will see how awful a person you are. You are never free to actually enjoy your own likes and dislikes as a man, instead you are constantly thinking about how others see you and if you will be accepted or not.

Jack, behind closed doors, inflicted a lot of pain on those around him, beating his children, messing with friends to breaking point, making jokes at their expense, and secretly plotting the horrible things he would do to his wife. "Push me one more time and I'll put you in the hospital," he said as his eyes burned.

On the outside, Jack proclaimed how good he was, how righteous he was, always desiring for the kind of harmony he never felt as a child. "I'm a really good guy," he shared with neighbors, or the police after a noise complaint about his screaming. As a child, Jack had been punished severely by his dad, who judged him and beat him. There was no escape from the torture; he saw his father as an evil man... but still as a man who loved him through these acts. Loved one second (in front of people) hated the next (behind closed doors). "It must be me," he concluded, while nursing his bruises. A part of Jack believed there was real love out there for him, but that hope had to be hidden away in the darkness, the void, the part of him he would just have to live with.

Cruelty, even in the most subtle forms, was a form of love for Jack. He attracted it into his relationships, just as much as he caused it. Inflicting pain and receiving pain was just as much an integral pattern in his life as eating and sleeping. His suffering would be the suffering of others, and haunt him for the rest of his life.

This is in no way an exhaustive list. There are more unnamed bullets than there are named ones. Anytime you blame yourself and give yourself a label, that is a bullet. This list of nine is simply some of the most common ones and a primer to help you see how they function. Yet at the end of the day, focus on the emotional work of actually pulling out bullets. If you simply overthink the bullets and mentally figure out which ones you have, you are wasting a lot of time and being unproductive. Those with the Stupid bullet typically avoid doing the actual emotional work, because they are telling themselves they are doing it wrong, and instead they just mentally investigate their bullets. That won't heal you and it won't heal your marriage, but it's a great way to waste a bunch of valuable time. Don't focus on the labels. Aim your energy at pulling out the suppressed emotion that came when you labeled yourself.

31
THE HARDEST THING YOU WILL EVER DO

First, let's review a few things about bullets. Bullets are a metaphor we use for a man's insecurities. Insecurities come from suppressed hurts, and a suppressed hurt is simply a past hurt that you have suppressed rather than letting out. After suppressing the hurt, you judged yourself ("I am stupid," "I am weak," "I am a loser," etc.). Lastly, you have then developed survival behaviors to hide and guard the suppressed hurt (control, yelling, avoiding, arguing, defending etc.) and this is where relationship-destroying behaviors come from.

WHERE DO BULLETS COME FROM?

1. CHILDHOOD BULLETS: AGES 4–21

These are the most dangerous ones and the average man has four to six deeper bullets with 10 to 15 different survival behaviors in each. The suppressed hurts typically first happened in childhood in connection with your mother, father or siblings. Other suppressed hurts include feeling bullied in school or sports, the death of a loved one, your parents divorcing or from physical and sexual abuse.

2. ADULTHOOD BULLETS: AGES 21–PRESENT

Most of these lead back to and are built on top of childhood bullets. Adulthood suppressed hurts can look like past relationship failures, past job failures and betrayals such as being cheated on.

3. FUTURE BULLETS

These are bullets that can develop from suppressing pain in the future rather than dealing with it responsibly. These only happen if you do not master releasing your emotion, and resort instead to suppressing it.

BULLETS ACTIVATE IN A VERY PREDICTABLE PATTERN

1. An external event happens which triggers the suppressed hurt.
2. You get angry, frustrated, resentful, or some other feeling related to anger.
3. You execute your survival behaviors (yelling, arguing, being defensive, name-calling, going silent, shutting down, etc.).

WHY IS IT IMPORTANT TO GET RID OF BULLETS?

Bullets cause you to give up self-control. They put you into fight, flight or freeze mode, which is another way of saying that your survival behaviors are trying to protect you from feeling the suppressed hurt, but as a result they damage your relationships.

When you are triggered, your bullets block you from allowing your wife to manage the relationship. You aren't functioning within the four-part structure of: your terms, cooperating with her management of the relationship, your purpose, your wants and feelings.

By being triggered, you are damaging the communication and

connection with your wife. You are sending her the message that you are insecure and cannot "be the bowl" or provide security for your family.

HOW TO PULL YOUR BULLETS

Pulling your bullets is an emotional process, not a logical one. The reason why all the things you have tried (counseling, books, blogs, online videos, therapists, men's groups, pastors, etc.) haven't worked is because they were based on logic.[12]

As a child, when you got hurt, you did not *think* your way into the hurt. You *felt* your way into it. You now have to feel your way out of it, using specific steps.

There are multiple ways to pull your bullets. You can learn about other ones when you join The Bulletproof Husband online, but here we will look at one of the most common and accessible methods.

PHYSICAL EXHAUSTION

This is the fastest way for 90% of men to pull bullets.

You have to begin by getting beyond anger. Anger, frustration and resentment are all bodyguards that are protecting you from feeling the suppressed hurt. You will have to get all the feelings of anger out before you are going to feel the suppressed hurt.

The first step is to get in a private environment with NO ONE around you and trigger yourself on purpose. You must intentionally feel the anger below the surface. Even make up an imaginary reason to be angry if you must (for example, imagine your wife having an affair in graphic detail – whatever it takes to get you explosively angry). When you get angry, get physically irresponsible. Absolutely lose it on a punching bag, or hit a wooden pallet with an axe, or try to rip the steering wheel out of your car. Also let out the anger with

12| It is easy for men to get stuck in logic, but you cannot "fix" your emotions by thinking your way out of them. The feminine typically is much more successful with current approaches to therapy because women need to talk out their bullets. The masculine needs to physically emote the suppressed emotions and most healing modalities do not create room for men to physically emote.

whatever sounds and words you need: yell, scream, call her names, or whatever you need to until the anger is all out. Continue until all the anger is physically exhausted.

Once the bodyguard of anger is out of the way, your suppressed hurt will begin to come to the surface as sadness and sorrow. Let yourself fully feel the sadness. Weep, cry, wail, gut yourself emotionally like a five-year old who had his candy stolen.[13]

Since the suppressed hurt is bubbling up from long ago, you may feel feelings from when you were four years old and your parents got divorced. Your brain will try to tell you that you are doing the process wrong. Yet it is very simple: if you are letting out anger and sadness, you are doing it right. Each time you let out more suppressed hurt, you are pulling out bullets and you will be less triggerable.

Warning: One of the side effects of bullets is the desire to "do it myself." Maybe this is because your bullets tell you that reaching out for help means you are "weak" or "stupid." When from another perspective, being able to get help means you are intelligent and strong enough to pull your mask down and be vulnerable. Don't waste time trying to pull all your bullets alone. Reach out and join The Bulletproof Husband program. We have a three-hour call every single week dedicated just to pulling bullets. Also we host men's retreats where some of the deepest bullets are pulled quickly and effectively.

A helpful context: Many men will avoid doing emotional work. Even men that are committed to saving their marriages will often quit doing emotional work when their wife takes them back. It is

13| Masssive Warning: I will repeat this whenever we are talking about letting out your emotions and pulling out your bullets. You must have high confidence before you start, otherwise the emotional work will actually drag you down into the depths of self-pity and self-blame. Pulling bullets while having low confidence can actually be dangerous for you mentally, emotionally and physically. After you complete doing emotional work, build your confidence back up again then move on with your day. The tools for managing your confidence can be found in the chapter entitled, "Got That Big D*ck Energy." Doing emotional work is one of the hardest things you will ever do and also one of the most important. For this reason alone, I would urge any man to join the Bulletproof Husband online program by going to www.BulletproofHusband.com/DocJon

vital that pulling bullets becomes a lifelong strategy for responsibly dealing with your masculine emotions. You are learning a skill that is intended to become a lifestyle. I challenge men with the picture of the peanut butter jar. I love peanut butter and there always comes a point where a normal person will throw out the empty jar, yet in my case, I am one of those "scrape the walls until every tiny bit of peanut butter has been eaten kind of guys." We must approach emotional work the same way. Be proactive until you have scraped your inner jar clean, this is the way to becoming your best and most solid self.

32
STOP BEING A MOMMA'S BOY

Being "complete" with your parents means that you have pulled all your bullets associated with them and hold zero blame toward them regarding your upbringing. You see them clearly as the flawed human beings that they are and accept them fully, and are actually thankful for how they raised you because you can see how they made you into the success that you are today.

The starting point for this can be varied. Say, for example, Bob sees himself as a loser *because of* his parents. He will have to dig out all the blame, hurt and anger he is holding toward his parents. On the other hand, Tim sees himself as successful *despite* his parents being harsh and abusive. Bob and Tim have different perspectives on themselves, but both will have to begin by digging out the suppressed hurt, anger and blame.

As the emotional work strips away the layers of suppressed hurt, there are five stages that each man passes through toward completion.

- **Idolization:** In our young childhood, we see our parents as basically superheroes.
- **Rebellion:** In our teen years, we see our parents as the authorities we must push against for freedom. Many people get stuck in this stage for their whole life and then act out rebelliously toward other authority figures.
- **Approval seeking:** In our early 20s, we want our parents to applaud us as we get our college degrees, earn at our successful career, have smart children, etc.
- **Acceptance:** In our 30s and 40s, we finally accept our parents as simply flawed human beings no different to ourselves.
- **Completion:** In our 40s to 60s, we watch our parents move close to their deathbed, and we finally face having to say our last words and leaving nothing unsaid.

It is not necessary to follow the timeline as laid out above. It is possible to do the emotional work at a much younger age and actually have a relationship where you hold zero blame toward your parents, where you accept them fully for the human beings that they are, and you have communicated everything and left nothing unsaid. Or, to say that another way, if they died tomorrow, you know that their job as a parent was complete and you needed nothing more from them and had nothing more to say to them.

Once you have arrived at that place of acceptance and completion, there is one more piece to the puzzle. If you are complete with your father, you will be able to see how he imparted to you the gift of masculinity. If you are complete with your mother, you will see how she imparted the gift of her unconditional love to you.

Often, it is best to go and have a one-on-one conversation where you share with them how you got rid of the blame you had been carrying, how you now accept them, how they did a good job, and how you are a successful man because of their contribution of the gift of masculinity or unconditional love.

In The Bulletproof Husband online program we help men walk through the five stages and arrive at a place to complete with each of their parents whether living or deceased. We can help you through this process.

33
HE TOUCHED YOU WHERE?!

Digging out the pain from a traumatic memory or event is very similar to dealing with bullets. The main difference is that trauma is like having a bullet that is surrounded with shame and avoidance strategies. One of the main avoidance strategies is to label the memory or event and classify it somehow. For example, "I was abused," "I was molested," "I was abandoned," etc. This seems to help mentally, yet it actually obscures the goal of doing emotional work. The labels often add to the drama and shame that surrounds the traumatic experience. Our goal here is to actually do the emotional work and make personal change.

Let's say, for example, that you have been doing the emotional work and pulling out your bullets, yet there is an area that you haven't made much progress in – let's use sexual shame, for example. Perhaps you are unwilling to pursue and initiate sex with your wife because you feel the fear of rejection and inadequacy. Every time you want to have sex with your wife, you also notice that you have a feeling that holds you back – you feel dirty and unlovable, so you are paralyzed and don't initiate. When you begin to dig into that feeling and where it came from, you remember that when you were six years old, you had a sexual encounter with your friend's older brother and that is where the original feeling of being dirty and unlovable came from.

Typically, a childhood memory like that gets labeled as "abuse" or "molestation" and is then avoided and pushed deep down in shame. *"I was sexually abused when I was six years old and that's why I can't..."* *(fill in the blank).*

Whatever happened in the past is now merely a fact. It is something that happened. It doesn't say anything about you; only your interpretation says something about who you are. The emotion that you continue to experience when you talk about that past story is a clear indicator of where you are at with your emotional work. If you are able to tell the facts of your story without the emotion, labeling or drama around it, you have reached a high level of emotional completion with yourself. If you are still telling your story filled with emotion and choking back tears while using lots of labels: "I was abused/molested/taken advantage of," then you have work to do. The goal is that you can tell a story that is simply the facts: "When I was six years old, my friend's older brother stuck his hand in my pants and squeezed my testicles several times."

A simple way to test how where you are at with your trauma is to ping-pong back and forth with another fact from the past that you have no emotion about.

For example:

- What did you have for breakfast this morning? *"Scrambled eggs and bacon."*
- What happened when you were six years old? *"My friend's older brother stuck his hand in my pants and squeezed my testicles several times."*
- What did you have for breakfast this morning? *"Scrambled eggs and bacon."*
- What happened when you were six years old? *"My*

friend's older brother stuck his hand in my pants and squeezed my testicles several times."

- What did you have for breakfast this morning? *"Scrambled eggs and bacon."*
- What happened when you were six years old? *"My friend's older brother stuck his hand in my pants and squeezed my testicles several times."*

If you can switch back and forth between what your last meal was and stating the facts of your traumatic event and say the facts without emotion and simply as something that happened that was as mundane as the scrambled eggs and bacon, then you have completed with the deep emotions that have been suppressed. If you are feeling emotion come up while you are trying to do this exercise, pause and let the emotion out: cry, scream, wail and do whatever you have to do to let the bullet, blame and pain out, then go back to the exercise.[14]

If you are solid at this level and want to test it at a higher level, look yourself in the eyes in a mirror and say your breakfast and your traumatic story with the same clarity, confidence and tonality, and a higher level would be to share your story with a male friend by telling him about the switching exercise and do this exercise with him several times.

When you are free of the blame, shame, emotion, trembling, hesitancy and labeling of your experience, you will be standing on the other side with major freedom from a deep, traumatic bullet.

14| Masssive Warning: I will repeat this whenever we are talking about letting out your emotions and pulling out your bullets. You must have high confidence before you start, otherwise the emotional work will actually drag you down into the depths of self-pity and self-blame. Pulling bullets while having low confidence can actually be dangerous for you mentally, emotionally and physically. After you complete doing emotional work, build your confidence back up again then move on with your day. The tools for managing your confidence can be found in the chapter entitled, "Got That Big D*ck Energy." Doing emotional work is one of the hardest things you will ever do and also one of the most important. For this reason alone, I would urge any man to join the Bulletproof Husband online program by going to www.BulletproofHusband.com/DocJon

34
DEPENDENTS ARE A LINE ON YOUR TAX FORM, NOT HOW YOU RUN A MARRIAGE

As an infant, each of us was wholly dependent on our caregivers. As we matured, we became independent and capable as individuals. This culminated in our being a contributor and participant in society, which is interdependent. The author Stephen Covey put it this way in his mega-bestseller:

On the maturity continuum, dependence is the paradigm of you – you take care of me; you come through for me; you didn't come through; I blame you for the results. Independence is the paradigm of I – I can do it; I am responsible; I am self-reliant; I can choose. Interdependence is the paradigm of we – we can do it; we can cooperate; we can combine our talents and abilities and create something greater together.

Dependent people need others to get what they want. Independent people can get what they want through their own effort. Interdependent people combine their own efforts with the efforts of others to achieve their greatest success.[15]

While the natural progression of maturity moves the individual through these three stages, emotional growth is often stunted and stuck in the first category. That first dependent stage, when it comes to emotions and relationships, is referred to as being codependent. It is that clingy, needy, approval-seeking Mr. Nice Guy syndrome. Many men are stuck in this stage of emotional maturity. And before they can be a solid, healthy, interdependent marriage partner, they first have to go on the journey from codependence to independence. When a man is truly independent, he is emotionally self-sufficient. That man accepts himself; he has integrated his past hurts and traumas, and he would change nothing about his upbringing because it all contributed to him being the successful man he is today. When you are able to say that you would change nothing in your past, you have arrived at this level of integration.

A self-sufficient man generates his own confidence and self-respect from within and does not seek outside sources of validation, but also doesn't turn them away out of insecure deflection when validation comes. The journey from being codependent to being independent involves mountains of emotional work, including pulling bullets, completing with parents, and desensitizing trauma. Once a man has become solidly self-sufficient, then he is quite a gem to be married to. He will be capable of being a contributor in an interdependent relationship. Many men arrive at independence and make statements like, "I feel so good about my life, I don't know if I even need a woman anymore!" And yes, at that point a man is faced with

---

15| Covey, Stephen R. "The 7 Habits of Highly Effective People: 30th Anniversary Edition" (p. 49). Simon & Schuster. Kindle Edition.

a choice. If he has children, then his commitment to his terms takes over and he will do all that is necessary to reconcile the relationship with his wife in the best interests of the children. If there are no children, then as he continues to be a high-value man, a man she would be a fool to leave, then over time she may choose to manage the relationship back together.

Consider this chapter as a roadmap. Are you codependent? Have you become emotionally self-sufficient? If so, are you ready to surrender to your terms and commitments, to give yourself over to an interdependent relationship? If you have gotten the slap, then these are three guideposts you will likely see on your way back to Stage Five.

35
WHICH IS BETTER, BEING BULLET-FREE OR BULLETPROOF?

I s the goal to be bullet-free or bulletproof? Well, actually, it is both, and they are different concepts.

Being bullet-free is the idea of having removed the bullets from your past, your childhood etc. This removal process for all the old, suppressed emotions being unearthed and released is usually quite extensive. Once a person has removed the old bullets that person becomes very hard to trigger in the present because they are not affected by a bunch of old bullets being poked. Also, they have a high level of self-acceptance.

Being bulletproof is about the ongoing emotional work. Every day, as we go through life, we face new opportunities to get new bullets. The bulletproof man keeps himself accountable and responsible for doing the emotional work to keep bullet holes from accumulating in his life. Another part of the bulletproof man is that he has done the emotional and practical work to be bulletproof in all the domains, which we will discuss in the last section of this book.

So do the work to become bullet-free, then keep doing the work to live as a bulletproof man.

SECTION RECAP

- Defining bullets: Also known as triggers, a bullet is a suppressed hurt which causes insecurity, which you then compensate for by doing survival behaviors.
- Triggers are your responsibility; you must own them and deal with them.
- Every bullet has a negative side, which creates insecurity, but then over-compensating for the insecurity creates an area of strength.
- Psych labels are sometimes disempowering cages; it can be much more helpful to just go with a universal label: "I was an asshole."
- There are nine major bullets: Stupid, Loser, Weak, Incompetent, Victim, Broken, Burden, Weird/Ugly/Different, Mean/selfish/Evil.
- You pull your bullets by physically emoting out the suppressed hurt.
- As you grow as a person, you go through five stages with your parents: Idolization, Rebellion, Approval seeking, Acceptance, Completion.
- Trauma is another way of saying, "a really deep bullet." It is released the same as any other bullet, except that a thick layer of shame usually accompanies it.

- We all are meant to mature through the three stages from Dependent to Independent to Interdependent.
- You have two goals, first become bullet-free from the past, then become bulletproof as you live in the present and future.

MEMBER STORY: SHE DIVORCED ME AND MOVED SEVEN DOORS DOWN

I can still remember that day almost six years ago when the time came for my wife and kids to move away. I sat in my front room on a bench that overlooks the front yard. I stepped outside to take it in. The air was crisp and I could smell the leaves as the weather was starting to turn from summer to fall. Tears welled up as they pulled away. My neighbor saw me and we wept together.

My world had collapsed. The crazy thing was she had found a house in the neighborhood SEVEN doors down. That's right, a one-minute walk. Hell, I could almost throw a rock and probably hit their house.

The feeling of being alone hit me like I had never felt before. Actually, that was just a lie I had been telling myself. You see, for 15 years of marriage and many years before that, I had been stuck in that dark place. Even though people I loved were there, I felt so alone. I had never dealt with the suppressed hurt from years of deriving false meanings about my abandonment issues regarding my dad and other hurt from childhood.

I jumped into another relationship pretty quickly after that. That empty feeling subsided, but it was temporary. Every time she would get upset or it felt like she might leave, those nagging issues of suppressed hurt would resurface. I hadn't learned to be alone. I didn't know the key to a successful relationship was loving myself first.

The relationship got off to a pretty rocky start. We had a birthday party for my youngest daughter. I wanted to prove to everyone that I had gotten over my ex-wife so I invited my new girlfriend to attend. She was reluctant, but I pushed her into a space that she wasn't ready to handle. But, in reality it was me who wasn't ready to handle it. I thought we could all be civil. I hadn't dealt with any of my bullets and a couple of weird looks from a friend of my ex-wife's (my friend too but now hers) and then a quick splash from my new girlfriend and I was triggered as fuck. Needless to say, I proceeded to make an ass of myself and ruined the party for everyone. Little did I know that even though I was able to patch things up with the woman I was dating, it was the nail in the coffin for any relationship with her since I had not completed with my ex-wife – and more importantly, with myself. I know my daughter took on a bullet that night. She still struggles with my ex-wife and me when it comes to the trust I am currently rebuilding there.

About a year, and countless arguments, getting defensive, hiding my feelings and so many other insecurities later, my girlfriend decided she had had enough. She left and I was crushed a second time. The fog that I was surrounded with during divorce resurfaced. Thankfully, I found TBH and the coaches here and countless other men helped me see where I was holding back and helped me dig into that emotional hurt. Being able to get to that place of hurt and pinpoint where it came from and recognize the triggers that take me back there help me know that my worth comes from what I do, outside of any relationship I am in.

Fast forward to the present. Five years from that low point of the party I ruined – the one where my ex-wife swore she'd never set foot in my house again – and I just pulled off an epic surprise party for my youngest daughter with the help of my ex-wife. It was the first time she had been at my house in over five years. Despite being mopey most of the day and even saying how she really didn't like birthday parties since people always get mad at them (I suspect she has internalized this due to my behavior five years ago) my daughter's eyes lit up like I hadn't seen in quite some time when we pulled off the surprise party! She ran around with her friends and came out of her shell, even though there was a convergence of two friend groups, and she deftly navigated all the possible teenage pitfalls that come with these activities. I may or may not have teared up a couple times. Perhaps we rewrote the script for the bullet she took from me five years ago!

Doing the work means I've been able to not only rebuild a great co-parenting relationship, but also has led to building a new relationship with my current girlfriend that is built on the principles of TBH, terms, cooperation with her management of the relationship, purpose and wants and desires. The relationship I am in now is the most fulfilling one I have experienced because it centers on the relationship I have with myself first. My relationship with my ex-wife and mother of my children is back on solid footing. My relationship with my kids is back to a place of leadership. My relationship with the woman I am with is building into a lifelong commitment.

Learn to love yourself. It may feel impossible, but if you do the work, you will get the results!!!

DEMYSTIFYING
THE EGO

36
EGO IS NOT THE ENEMY

There have been brilliant authors and Eastern philosophical traditions I highly respect that have taken a negative stance toward the ego. I am going to give a different perspective here for you to consider, and rather than writing volumes on the subject, I am going to be direct. I don't believe that ego is your enemy. Arrogance, pride and hubris are enemies to watch out for, but I would lean toward Carl Jung's perspective of the ego, as described in his masterful work "Aion: Researches into the Phenomenology of the Self."

Carl Jung considered the ego to be part of a larger whole known as the self, and the ego to be specifically related to our self-aware conscious choices and personality, whereas the self was larger and encompassed other arenas such as the unconscious and subconscious.

Here's where the rubber meets the road: if your *ego* is the problem, then you have an unsolvable problem and you are going to struggle with it until death. However, if your *bullets* are the problem, then you can address those proactively, pull them out, and have a healthy functional ego. Let's use the terminology of the author

Eckhart Tolle and say that each person has an invisible "pain body" which accumulates all the bullet holes we have received over the years. If we do the emotional work to remove those bullets, then that invisible body is once again strong and healthy.

This perspective gives room to the idea that you can actually make progress, remove bullets and live a life with a healthy powerful ego that makes a difference in this world. This will require that we let go of the modern myth that ego means arrogance, pride or hubris, and begin to see the ego as a neutral container of our self-aware personality. It also requires that we do the work to pull out the buried hurt within that ego container, and then live our life through a healthy functional ego.

37
NICE GUYS, TRIGGERS AND EGOS, OH MY!

Don't make it your goal to never trigger other people.

Make it your goal to be your authentic self. The YOU who you are without any bullets. The YOU who is complete with your parents. The YOU who has delivered all the BPAs necessary to be complete with yourself. The real YOU who is actually your healthy bullet-free ego.

The you who is afraid of triggering your wife or others is actually still the bullet-ridden version of you. It is the you who wants to be liked and accepted by everyone. The you who will change yourself and play the game just to gain a crumb of approval, as you live tip-toeing around on eggshells.

If you are still trying to be liked, trying to win the approval of others, or hiding parts of yourself to be accepted, then you are being a "nice guy" and you are being inauthentic. And eventually, when your willpower runs out, your suppressed feelings will bubble to the surface and you will lash out at others. You likely have a deep well of suppressed rage from feeling wronged by others. You aren't even authentically nice; you simply play nice as a manipulation tactic so that you can receive acceptance and love.

The nice guy is actually just one form the bullet-ridden ego takes. If your ego is full of suppressed emotion and bullets, then your ego is sick, weak and infected, just like any physical body would be if it were shot up with bullets. As we saw in the previous chapter, ego is NOT the enemy; a weak ego is actually a dangerous one. It is the man with a bullet-riddled ego who will be lying, hiding himself, manipulating, being controlling and putting heavy expectations on others. A healthy ego has no need to do any of those things.

What if you had a healthy ego and actually chose to be unapologetically yourself? What if you accepted yourself fully, and grew your self-trust and self-respect to the level where you didn't need to get those from an outside source? What if you didn't emotionally need anything from others? What if their affirmation, acceptance or pats on the head for being a good little boy no longer held any sway over you? What if you simply never thought about love languages ever again and just accepted yourself, lived your terms and let others manage their relationship with you? You would never again be calculating in your head: "I did this for her, so she should reciprocate to meet my needs!"

Would that authentic YOU still trigger your wife and others at times? Absolutely. But would you have anything to apologize for? Hell, no. Those are their triggers and not your responsibility.

Have you taken 100% responsibility for yourself? Are you managing your own confidence and being solid? Are you connected with a tribe that will hold you accountable for being in integrity? Are you maintaining high levels of self-trust and self-respect? If the answer is yes to all of the above, then you will definitely trigger others when you unabashedly speak from your heart, but you will have nothing to regret and nothing to hide. Any man who is managing his life in this way is actually inspiring to others, and the world longs for any man who is responsible and authentic on that level. Once you are operating at that level, if you *choose* to take responsibility for the feelings and needs of others, that is where leadership begins. As my co-author Dr. Gary Menezes says, "Leadership begins when you are taking responsibility for what you aren't seen as responsible for."

Warning: The goal is to become the man YOU'VE always wanted to be, not to become the man your WIFE has always wanted you to be. If you simply become what she wants, you are not being authentic, you are approval seeking and actually being manipulative.

38
ARE YOU WINNING AGAINST YOUR WIFE?

Let's begin with a brief review of masculine and feminine energies. Every person, whether male or female, gay or straight, all have both masculine and feminine energies within them. Typically, most men have a masculine inner core and most women have a feminine inner core, yet there is a balancing act between the two energies within each of us.

Now to dig deeper, the ego is larger within the masculine energy side of each person. It is part of what drives competition, whether in sports, the military or the workplace. The masculine ego is a powerful, useful force in the right arenas. However, it is important to understand that the ego must never be a part of your marriage relationship. The ego is not relational by nature – it is competitive. So bringing the ego into your marriage will only create competition and conflict.

In managing the relationship, your wife will also manage your ego at times. If you come home from closing a big deal at work and your ego feels huge and powerful, she will test, poke and prod at you. She will make sure that your ego doesn't turn into hubris and arrogance, which would actually hurt both of you. On the flip side, if you come home from a really crappy day where your boss has shouted at you and you have failed at several tasks, your ego will be really deflated. On days like that, she will likely build up your ego. She will remind you of better days and your past accomplishments. There is a careful balance here – although it feels really good to have her boost up your ego, don't become reliant on her doing that. Long-term, it will exhaust her if you aren't being self-sufficient. Also, if you want to keep increasing your confidence level and ego power, you will need to boost her ego up to meet you at your level, rather than having her pull your ego down. To raise her ego to meet you at a higher level will require a high level of leadership from you.

In summary of the last three chapters, we have seen that pulling out your bullets will make your ego healthy and functional. You will then be able to use the power of your ego to compete and achieve great things in life. At times, your wife will manage your ego to keep you out of arrogance or depression, which are both dangerous to the marriage.

Last, make sure that you don't bring ego into your marriage: it isn't a competition and only a bullet-riddled insecure man would feel the need to be competing with his own wife.

SECTION RECAP

- Ego is NOT the enemy: Your bullets that are lodged in your "pain body" are the real issue. You are not in an endless struggle with your ego,
- Nice guys, triggers, and egos, oh my! Be your authentic self, even if it triggers other people. The goal is the be the man you've always wanted to be, not to be the man everyone else has always wanted you to be.
- Keep your ego out of the marriage: Your wife is your teammate, not your competition.

MEMBER STORY: 4 FEET TALL WITH A HUGE EGO TO 15 FEET TALL AND HUMBLE

Today I walk around feeling 15 feet tall with my head held high at any moment. However, just a few years ago it was not this way.

A few years ago, I can vividly recall when I felt four feet tall.

My house was silent. I was curled up in a ball in a single bed in the dark basement. I could not see much more than a few feet in front of me. The only glimmer of light was from the top of the stairs. The musty smell of the basement was getting to me. It was 12:45 AM. I had tears flowing down my face.

In that moment I made a decision. A decision that would change my life forever. A decision that would lead me to the greatest version of myself. A decision that I would not have believed possible 12 months prior.

You see, just a short 12 months prior, I had been dealing with my wife asking for a separation. I'd thought that this was the end – the end of my marriage, the end of my family, the end of my happiness, and ultimately the end of my life.

I knew I had made many mistakes. I had yelled at my wife and kids. I knew I had not been present for them. However I believed that I deserved another chance.

However, I was still acting like I was dependent upon my wife and needy for attention. Ultimately, the courts determined that we needed a nesting arrangement until the separation was finalized.

Fortunately, that night in the basement, I made a decision. I took action to never return to the man I had been in the past and become a man who is powerful and serves his purpose.

Fortunately, rather than focusing on my complaints about others, one of my coaches held me responsible. He provided tough love to get me to take responsibility for my actions. He held me accountable for the hurt and pain I had caused in others.

Openly, I actually felt better as I was moving towards the best version of myself. I felt that my confidence was sky high and I was a powerful man. I did the work to become the best version of myself. I dealt with the pain and hurt of my past. I even realized what I needed to be in order to be ready for a deep loving relationship.

The decision I made started me down the journey to transform from a four-foot version of myself to become the best version of myself. I joined TBH in January 2020, attended the retreat in February 2020 and dug in by doing the work, delivering BPAs and focusing on thriving in all domains of my life.

Today, I stand 15 feet tall, head up and breathing in the fresh air. Shining my light for all. I live to serve with gratitude for every moment.

My best version is alive now.

My best version is a Warrior of Light who stands 15 feet tall.

DEALING WITH
THE FEMININE

39
SHE'S NOT DELUSIONAL, JUST GIVE HER FIVE MINUTES

The legend goes that there were five men who had been blind since birth. These men had never seen an elephant and each of them was taken to an elephant and allowed to feel one part of the elephant: an ear, the tail, a tusk, the trunk and a leg. Then they were asked to describe the elephant. Each man described what he had felt with his hands, and of course each one described something different: the man who touched the leg said that the elephant was like a tree trunk. The man who touched the tail said an elephant was like a rope. The man who touched the tusks said the elephant was like a spear, and so on. None of them were actually wrong. Each man was correct in what he described. It was just that they each had a different experience of the elephant, and could only describe that part.

"The Elephant and the Five Blind Men" is similar to the masculine trying to understand the feminine. The masculine and feminine perspectives of the world are as far apart as a man looking up at a sky and saying, "Look, a blue sky!" and the woman next to him saying, "No, it's a pink sky!" It doesn't matter if that man provides a dozen articles saying the sky is blue, if his therapist agrees that it's blue, if science confirms that it's blue, or if "everyone knows" it's blue. If she feels it is pink, that's what she is going to believe, end of story.

The goal is not to change her mind, especially by reasoning or arguing with her. Also, don't compromise by meeting in the middle with something like: "Well, maybe the sky isn't blue or pink; maybe it's a mixture, which means it's purple." The feminine doesn't feel safe with the masculine when it folds and compromises, nor when he tries to convince, control or gaslight her into seeing the sky as blue. Instead, be solid. Know that the sky looks blue to you, and don't go into judgment of her view. Instead, get curious and dig into her perspective. "Oh, the sky looks pink to you? What shade? Is it light pink or neon pink or hot pink? How do you feel about the sky being pink?" With the feminine, it is rarely about coming to a conclusion or agreement; the real goal is having her express her experience, her perspective, and for her to then feel heard.

Remember the principle: Women feel and then act; men act and then feel. When she is claiming the sky is pink, it is because she feels it is pink. If she expresses herself and then feels heard, understood, appreciated and valued, then the sky color can shift for her. After a deep sigh of relief from feeling HUAVed, she may say something like, "Thank you for listening to me. Perhaps the sky actually is blue, or red, or yellow." After she has expressed herself and has felt heard through your response, her feelings will be able to shift, which will lead to her perspective being able to shift.

It doesn't matter if she is saying, "You are a narcissistic, grooming, gas-lighting, predator sex-addict. I will never have feelings for you again. I will never trust you again. You are an abuser." All she's really saying is, "Will you please listen to my deeper feelings beyond my splashy emotional surface and hear the pain I am feeling? The fear and distrust I am feeling? I am trusting you and pleading for you to show up solid for me and help me get this out." Each time you listen through the splashing, you are taking a thimbleful of poison out of her bucketful of hurt feelings. Stop getting hung up on the difference in perspective. You lead your marriage through listening. It only seems true to her because she is feeling that way in the moment. For those in the feminine, truth shifts moment by moment as their feelings shift.

She may stomp, yell and scream that the sky is pink for five minutes, and if you listen well, five minutes later she may be saying, "Actually, I think it does look blue; maybe you're right." As Tony Robbins says, "All change is a change of feelings." Said another way, the ability to master masculine listening will give you marriage leadership superpowers.

40
ARE YOU HER PUNCHING BAG?

When you are punching a punching bag and working on pulling bullets, you are stripping out layers of suppressed hurt. This often includes screaming, crying, blaming, cursing, calling your wife (or mom, uncle, coach etc.) every name in the book. Your wife's process of pulling bullets is basically the same, except you are her punching bag and her punching is going to be verbal.

For the feminine to get her bullets out, she must verbally process her pain, blame, anger etc. This is why therapy is much more effective for women because it is geared for the feminine verbal processor (whereas the masculine heals through physically emoting the pain).

For the victim-minded man who hasn't been trained to understand the difference between the masculine and feminine, it would seem that his wife is verbally abusing him. Actually, she is trusting and relying on him to help her get her bullets out. You may be thinking, "But she has been bitching for years; why aren't her bullets out by now?! I can't believe this will ever stop." The reality is that she will continue complaining about the same stuff endlessly until you use HUAV, OEQs and BPAs to draw the pain out and help her feel heard, understood, appreciated and valued.

There may be things you have heard her complain and vent about for decades, but once you deliver a Full Bulletproof Apology, they will disappear and you will never hear about them again.

Many men want respect from their wife and feel like they are driven crazy by their wife's nagging and complaints. Then some other sweet young thang comes along who doesn't complain and nag – in fact, she gives him respect and boosts his ego up, and that's where a lot of affairs start. Yet at the end of the day, no matter what woman you end up with, eventually her bullets will build up and she will need to verbally process. If you just keep replacing the woman rather than learning the skills to help her verbally remove her bullets, that's how you will end up with two, three and four divorces as a man.

The best thing you can do for your children is learn how to help your wife get her bullets out. Also, when you help her get a bullet out, her respect for you actually increases, which is a bonus win.

Here it is in a metaphor: in The Bulletproof Husband, we sometimes refer to a woman verbally processing her bullets as "letting out venom." To the new guys, they picture it as being some sort of cowering bunny and their wife is some sort of coiled cobra ready to sink her fangs into them. This is not the right perspective. That's actually a victim mindset; it's already being on the defensive and setting themselves up to fail at being the bowl.

Here's a more mature masculine picture: your wife is a soft, sweet bunny rabbit, and she has fang marks all over her where you as a rattlesnake have bitten her for years. Your fangs have pumped venom into her. Yes, in your imagination she has been throwing that venom back at you, but the reality is that the poor bunny has to squeeze that venom out of herself to get free of it and get healthy again. From here forward, your goal is to no longer be a rattlesnake, to never bite her again and to actually show up as a veterinarian to help her get that venom out.

We punch punching bags to get our bullets out, but we show up as a punching bag to help her get her bullets out. Be a solid bowl and let her splash until she gets it out.

41
BUT SHE'S THE ONE CHEATING!

How do you take 100% responsibility when she is the one cheating? As Tony Robbins often says to men at his Date With Destiny events, "You have to own that you broke your vows first." Now perhaps your Loser bullet will be poked and you'll start saying, "That's not fair!" And it's not. So what? Listen up, buttercup: who promised you that life would be fair? Sometimes life is like a box of chocolates; sometimes it's like masturbating with calloused hands – it's rough.

When you and your wife stood at the altar and made vows to each other, you each heard different things. The typical man heard her promise that she would physically give herself to him and sexually be his forever. The typical woman heard him say that he would be her safe place and emotionally take care of her heart forever.[16]

Imagine that six months after marrying you, your wife comes home one day, opens the fridge and it's empty. She checks the pantry: empty. The cupboards: empty. The basement and the garage: empty. Not one crumb of food remains in the house. She is confused, upset and getting hungry. She calls you and starts yelling about the

16| He heard "Forsaking all others." She heard "I will love, honor and cherish."

food. You argue, deflect and defend. Ultimately, she gets in her car and goes to the grocery store and fills the trunk of her car with bags of food. When she comes home, she doesn't tell you that there are groceries in her car. In fact, she keeps it hidden. She thinks to herself, "I have to eat. I have to take care of *myself*. He said he would take care of me, but clearly he isn't."

One day, you open the trunk of her car and find all this food. You are upset and start yelling, "How could you? It is my job to feed you! I can't believe you would go out and get your own groceries!"

When a woman is sexually unfaithful to the marriage, typically her man has not provided emotionally for her heart for a long time. A woman's emotional needs are nearly on the level of physical hunger needs. If you aren't taking care of them, then she is forced to take action herself. When you committed to her in marriage, you committed to take care of those emotional needs. Perhaps her morals and ethics will keep her from having a physical affair, but she will entangle herself emotionally to get those needs met. And when another man makes himself available to listen to her and meet those emotional needs, it's usually only a matter of time before she feels obligated to give back to him in some sort of physical/sexual way.

Once you own the responsibility for her emotional needs, you will refill the fridge, the cupboards, the pantry and begin laying out a feast on the dining table each night for dinner. Yet she will probably keep her trunk full of food for a while. She will sit cautiously for dinner. She will be anxious each day, not sure if the food will run out. It will take time and consistency for her trust to be restored. Eventually, she will be able to stop buying her own groceries and she will know that she can rely on you again.

Looking at it from this perspective can free you from the victim mindset and show how you are 100% responsible for the state of the relationship. Now get to work on filling those cupboards through helping her feel heard, understood, appreciated and valued (HUAV).

42
STOP BEING VULNERABLE!

Imagine a knight in medieval times wearing a suit of armor. After a brutal battle, he lifts up a section of his armor to reveal a bloody gash. That injured area is a place where he is vulnerable. To reveal that gash, he must first have trust in the person he reveals it to. It would be unwise for him to expose the wound to a person who is going to heartlessly jab their finger into the cut. Yet that is often what men do with their vulnerability. Once they get the slap, they start doing introspective work and they begin to share their vulnerabilities with friends and extended family. Sometimes they even try to share with the wife who just slapped them! This is a terrible idea; she is hurt, angry and checked out.

From Stage Zero until you are deep into Stage Three, it is best to share your vulnerabilities with your tribe of men. Let them be the ones you process with. Your extended family and friends are prone to picking sides and giving lopsided, biased advice when you share your vulnerabilities. But your tribe of men are going to challenge you to be the man you have always wanted to be, to be 100% responsible, 100% trusting, to have zero expectations, to do the emotional work, to live by your terms and to be the man you want your sons to be and your daughters to marry.

Typically your friends and family want to give you comfort and encouragement, yet when you have a big gash in your side under your armor, you need men who will hold you down and sew you up. It will hurt like crazy sometimes, but it isn't meant to harm you. There is a huge difference between *hurt* and *harm*. When the dentist extracts a tooth, it hurts you, but it doesn't harm you. When you work out at the gym, your muscles may hurt, but it doesn't harm you. In the same way, we each need a tribe of men who are willing to hear our vulnerabilities and challenge us in a way that hurts us – this is how we heal and grow.

Once your relationship with your wife has made it back to late Stage Three, you can begin to reveal your vulnerabilities, and she can even poke at them, which will be a part of her testing you and rebuilding trust.

When you reveal your vulnerabilities, you are offering a step toward *intimacy*. One way that intimacy is built is by vulnerabilities being shared. As a man, you must be careful not to share your vulnerabilities with women outside your marriage. It will likely create emotional connections that endanger your terms and your integrity as a husband and father. Your terms are best served if you reserve your vulnerabilities for your intimate relationships such as your wife and your tribe of men.

43
REJECTION IS HER SUPERPOWER

The typical Mr. Nice Guy pleaser considers being rejected to be possibly the most painful experience he can have emotionally. This leads him to do all he can to avoid experiencing rejection. Yet once he begins pulling bullets and living a masculine life, an entirely different reality becomes available. A reality where rejection is simply a part of the masculine/feminine dance, not something crippling.

When a woman rejects a man, it may have been a test to poke him to see if he has insecurities and bullets. If he takes the rejection personally and collapses internally, she knows that she has avoided continuing a dangerous relationship with an insecure man. But if a man has previously dealt with his bullets, then her rejection becomes an opportunity to build the spark in the relationship. Then, when she pushes him away and he solidly listens and then injects some confident humor into the situation, she may be rattled and often opens up rather than continuing the rejection.

Another way to understand this is that rejection actually gives her a feeling of power in the relationship. Each time she is able to reject you while you remain solid, you are giving her a gift of feeling self-controlled and powerful in the relationship. Sex is a clear example of this. There are nights where I say, "Hey babe, I want to have sex with you tonight." On occasion she might say, "I am really stressed out and not up for it tonight." In the past, as an insecure nice guy, I would have felt deeply rejected and wounded for having stuck my neck out so far. I would have chastised myself for being so direct, on the rare occasions I was ever that direct as a nice guy. Now as a bulletproof man, I am direct and I don't take rejection personally. So if she tosses out the rejection above, I would likely come back with, "Ok babe, just know that I want to have sex with you and I will rock your world whenever you are ready." I will then move on with my evening. I go do something purposeful or watch a movie by myself, etc. Typically, those rare rejections are then turned around because like most women, she is turned on by a confident, purposeful man who passes the rejection test by remaining solid.

Give her the gift of being able to reject you without your ego collapsing. It will make her feel powerful and create attraction toward you.

44
KILL YOUR INNER NICE GUY

A pleaser: on paper, that does not seem like something morally incorrect or a character trait to be ashamed of. In reality, being a pleaser, and specifically a people pleaser, can be defined as "someone who tries hard to make others happy." It still does not appear to be too big an issue until you learn that people pleasers often act out of an insecurity or low self-esteem.

So what is the secondary gain to being a people pleaser? Why would people do that or be that? Well one of the many reasons and many secondary gains is that they actually end up feeling needed and being of use – typically these are considerable gains for a person habitually acting from a place of low self-esteem. A people pleaser will almost literally do anything in the search of that external validation because they so badly need it.

At this stage of the book, it should be clear to you that The Bulletproof Husband does not impose its meaning of right and wrong; TBH simply recognizes that the definitions of right and wrong are based on the perspective of the individual defining them. I highlight this so that you can be clear: it is not wrong to be a people pleaser.

What we do want to address is *why* an individual is a people pleaser and whether it is coming from a place of power or not. Realizing you are a people pleaser as a result of bullets and insecurities actually gives you an access point to powerfully address those insecurities and alter the behavior.

Why would it even be considered a negative in a marriage or long-term relationship to be a people pleaser? Surely to care so much about your loved one and be willing to sacrifice yourself and your happiness would be the foundation of a loving and long-lasting relationship? Actually, no: the danger occurs when you fail to get the recognition or validation you expect. The danger occurs when you feel how unfair it is that you are constantly there for them yet they often say no to you. The danger occurs when you start to resent them for who they are because of your dissatisfaction with yourself regarding who you are.

Being helpful is a slightly different concept to being a people pleaser. Not only is it a different concept, but it also has different consequences. Typically, for men, being helpful is being a fixer. By being helpful, it is almost predictably certain that you will want to rush in, uninvited, and fix your wife's or partner's problem. The real problem being that she didn't ask you to fix it – unless she specifically asks you to do so. In fact, what she has really done is shared with you about an aspect of her life which isn't working or she has some feelings around, and needs her feelings to be recognized.

If you don't realize this, then you being helpful can often be viewed as being invasive and this is particularly clear when the need to fix something quickly will actually kill your connection or under-standing of where your wife is at. If you are one of those people who is currently thinking, "Now I am being punished for being helpful?", well, then I am confident in telling you that you still have emotional work to do and that you have missed a vital differentiator: balance! Being helpful is a great trait in any human. Being overly helpful to the point where you are constantly trying to fix, impose your view on how a situation should be fixed, or robbing someone of the opportunity for growth – and in doing so, communicating that you don't believe the other person can resolve something on their own intelligence and life experience... well, that is when being helpful is out of balance!

So where is the balance? The balance is in "being of service" to your wife or partner. When you have done the emotional work around being a people pleaser or being helpful, it clears the way for you to be of service. By being of service, you can actually be there for your wife or partner based on *their* needs and not based on *your* needs as a result of your insecurities. Take the simple metaphor of a waiter or waitress: they are there to serve you, to facilitate you in getting what *you* want or need, not what they *feel* you need, as you take your seat.

You can also look at this as serving a higher power. Whether you already serve a spiritual higher power or a higher power in the context of someone serving their country, you too can serve the higher power of the marriage or relationship by being of service to your wife or partner. Being of service can be achieved without placing expectations on the other person and merely by being who you are.

As always, being of service should not come at the cost of you losing your commitment to your terms – unless of course you allow that to happen by not being the man you have always needed to be.

45
SHE'S UNHAPPY —
SO WHAT?

In this wonderful age of buzz words, words like "synergy," "new normal," "take this offline," and "circle back," one which also comes to mind is "self-care." Self-care has become the universal antidote for lacking happiness.

"Not happy enough? What you need is more self-care!"

In reality, happiness is a choice. Not only is it a choice, but it's a choice each individual makes for themselves and is responsible for making.

I recall a quote from Eleanor Roosevelt: "No one can make you feel inferior without your consent." It really is a powerful quote when you break down the components of it.

"No one can make you feel…" think about that. Your feelings are YOUR feelings. They can be influenced by others, yes, but they still remain *your* feelings.

The second component is "…without your consent." *You* are the one who signs off on how you feel. You give it the thumbs up or thumbs down.

Let's put this into a real life, everyday occurrence. How is it that at a funeral, some people celebrate the life that was, while others mourn the loss? The same situation – different feelings for different people. Feelings are the result of many factors, including education, the environment in which you were raised, role models in your life and natural personality, to mention but a few.

Within the context of a marriage or a committed relationship, there are two substantial eureka moments available. When you come to understand that (1) your happiness is your responsibility, and (2) your wife or partner's happiness is their responsibility.

All those times you may have said, "She just doesn't make me happy anymore," or "Why can't she just be happy? I do so much for her!" Those two sentences speak to a dependency you have on her for your happiness, and to your unmet expectations of her response to you. They also speak to the controlling nature of you trying to "fix" her. Happiness is a choice: your choice in relation to you and her choice in relation to her.

Depending on your bullets and your personality, you may find it difficult to separate yourself from the responsibility of her happiness. If you are a pleaser, you will want to, and likely have been, trying to please her and others in your life. You will almost do anything to avoid her thinking badly of you. You will sacrifice your wellbeing by not being, well, responsible for yourself.

What happens when you feel you don't deserve to be happy? Will you gravitate toward those who are also not happy for whatever reason? In your place of responsibility, you must do the work necessary to deal with your bullets and your baggage.

While you are not responsible for her happiness or feelings in general, you do have responsibilities. You are responsible for providing a safe place for your wife or partner to be able to express her feelings. You are responsible for the impact of your actions and behavior. You are responsible for taking ownership when she holds up the mirror to show you the impact of your actions. If you were to dismiss this responsibility, you would effectively be communicating

"Hey honey, your emotions are your emotions to figure out; let me know when you are good!" You cannot be oblivious to her hurt, anger, pain, sadness, happiness, joy, gratitude etc.

As you take it all in that you are not responsible for her happiness, or any of her emotions, look closely at why you held that belief in the first place. Who gave it to you? How long have you been living with it? How long have you been trying to fix others' emotions, robbing them of the opportunity of growth? What other relationships are affected by you being responsible for another person's feelings?

Now, moving forward, bring your awareness to that temptation to fix and resist it. This is another muscle you need to train after doing the relevant emotional work on your part to deal with associated bullets.

Then, meet her where she is at by being solid, consistent and reliable.

46
HELP, I'M MARRIED TO BRUCE WILLIS!

Perhaps you have seen that there are times when your wife seems masculine. Her communication is direct and short. She is callous and not caring. She seems checked out and distant, with minimal affection. She demonstrates anger and frustration. Some men will go as far as saying, "My wife is an alpha female." What they mean is that she behaves in a masculine way very often. It even seems like it is her natural way of being.

Of course, there are women who are more masculine than others. This can happen for several reasons. The way she was brought up is one. Perhaps, raised by an alpha male father who was hard on her to ensure she was prepared for life or because he always wanted a boy and decided to raise his daughter as one. Perhaps she was surrounded by many brothers and, being the only female, masculine traits rubbed off on her. Another scenario could be the workforce. She could be going to a male-dominated nine-to-five environment, spending most of her time there. When she arrives home, she still operates in that mode. These are all possible reasons why she is operating from a masculine place during any given time. However, this is far from being the whole picture.

Women can manage relationships from the feminine essence or from the masculine. Managing from the feminine means they are using their feelings and intuition to manage your feelings and hence where the relationship is going. However, when she manages from the masculine, it's direct and straight to the point. For example, when she makes a very specific request of you to do something around the house. What happens when her way of being is dominantly masculine? Is it really that she is an alpha female? Is it really about her not knowing the feminine because of how she was raised? Well, not exactly. Her habitual being may have been masculine, but her natural inclination will always be to the feminine.

So why does your wife have a hard time being feminine then? The feminine and masculine are polar opposites. Which means that they attract each other like magnets. If you are being your masculine true self, it creates the space for her to be her feminine true self. However, when you as a man start to diverge from your path of masculinity, your wife's space and feeling of safety to be feminine becomes threatened. When this happens, her management of the relationship starts to shift more toward the masculine because she now has to overcompensate for the lack of masculinity on your end in the relationship.

Again, it cannot be stressed enough how well your wife can manage the relationship (even when to you it doesn't make sense). If she senses your lack of masculinity on a consistent basis, she will then come in and overcompensate to make up for it in the relationship. At this point, you have to realize the following: if you are being less masculine and she has to make up for it by being more masculine, then this means you are being more feminine. Which makes sense, given that you only have two options. Hence, if you are not being masculine, it must be that you are being feminine. If she is over-compensating by being masculine, then she is being less feminine.

Another important fact that must be highlighted is that this doesn't happen overnight. It is a gradual breakdown into depolarization. Your masculine becomes weak while your feminine becomes stronger and her feminine becomes weak while her masculine becomes stronger. You start to cancel each other out by becoming neutral. Attraction stops and the relationship breaks down.

Add on top of the scenarios previously mentioned – the habitual behaviors from how she was raised or even the work environment in a male-dominated field. If depolarization has already started to happen AND she works in a masculine environment, it is much easier for her to stay masculine because she doesn't have the space to feel feminine at home and she is already wearing the masculine hat.

You will have to intentionally grow and become more masculine, so that when she comes home, she can switch into her feminine and know that you will provide the masculine that the relationship environment needs.

Also, when she doesn't feel safe in the relationship, she may switch into masculine mode and begin to give you orders: "I want you to get all your shit out of my house by 7pm on Friday." When it is clear, direct, and specific, she is being masculine and the best approach is to do exactly as she says. This is completely different to when she is being feminine and splashy and says something emotional but non-specific: "We aren't a good fit; I think we should break up and you should move out." This isn't a command, and it isn't masculine; it is an opportunity to listen, HUAV and OEQ.

47
IT'S HER GLASS CEILING AND YOU DON'T HAVE A HAMMER

Have you ever had the experience where you are really trying to express your love and appreciation to your wife, yet it gets constantly rejected? No matter how hard you want to express it to her, she is just reluctant to accept it from you. For a man, this is really difficult to comprehend because oftentimes, her actions and words would suggest that that is exactly what she wants. Yet, when you go and deliver, not only does it not serve the purpose but oftentimes makes things much worse, and you can even end up in an argument. Why does this happen? Why are her actions and words so contradictory to each other? The simple answer is this: *you can never love a woman more than she loves herself.*

Let's elaborate on this so that you have a better understanding. The average woman's self-esteem is naturally lower than that of an average man's self-esteem. This is not because women are weaker than men. In fact, outside of natural physical strength, the average woman is stronger than an average man in many regards. Pain tolerance, for example. The average man would not be able to bear the pain of childbirth. Relationship skills are another example. Most men do not have the strength and skillset to nurture relationships to the degree that women can. Emotional intelligence is yet another example. The EQ of women is far more advanced than that of men. All this is to highlight that neither is wrong or right. It simply comes down to understanding and appreciating the beautiful differences and uniqueness both bring to the table.

Just like many other character traits of feminine and masculine, the evolution of self-esteem for each of these started thousands of years ago when men were hunters and women were gatherers. To put this in very simple terms, a woman did not need to have a high degree of self-esteem to gather berries, to tend to the children and to cook. What was required of them included relationship skills, nurturing skills, intuitive skills and culinary skills. On the other hand, when men went to hunt for food or to fight off a saber-tooth tiger, a high degree of self-esteem was a necessity to survive and to bring food back to the village. Putting emotions aside and not bottling them up was a must in order to remain focused during the hunt and ensure they returned to the family. As men took on these roles at the beginning of mankind, their self-esteem and the confidence surrounding it was strengthened and ingrained in the masculine traits of men.

What you might be thinking now is the comparison to today's world. In modern society, one might argue this is not the case anymore. Women work out, women lead companies, women fight in the UFC and women do many other "masculine" roles that require a high degree of self-esteem. This is true. So is the reverse. Men do more cooking, more child-raising and other... what one might call *feminine-denominated* roles. This phenomenon of equalizing the feminine/masculine roles between men and women is driven by societal changes and the evolution of humanity within it. All fantastic and long-awaited. However, what we are talking about here is the previous thousands of years which has genetically ingrained in men and women traits that cannot be disregarded and will take just as long to shift more permanently (long after you are gone from Earth). This also applies to self-esteem. The natural self-esteem of a husband and wife will be different. Assuming we are aligned on the above, you can now see that when you, the husband, with a naturally higher self-esteem, attempt to present your wife in a view that is not consistent with her own self-image, she will have a very difficult time accepting it.

What is your level of confidence and self-esteem regarding sitting in a space shuttle, navigating it and then going out to space? Unless you are a trained astronaut reading this book, the odds are very low that your self-esteem is high in this regard. But then, I come to you and attempt to make you believe that you are capable of doing this mission – indeed you can navigate this shuttle and go to space. Would you accept it just because I said it? Would it frustrate you that I am trying to convince you of something that is not true? Could you end up in an argument with me by becoming more and more frustrated? Would it alter your view of yourself just because I am saying those "confidence-boosting lines" to you? Do you see where this is going?

Oftentimes a husband wants to fix his wife's feelings and view of herself. He wants to manage her feelings, thinking that he knows how. It never works because it is not his job to do so. He cannot want it more than she does. This also goes for showering your wife with the love and affection that she may not feel she deserves, because her self-esteem is in a place where it cannot receive all that. It cannot take in all that.

The solution is to control what you can control and let her have control of herself. Yes, it will require your patience and it is on her timeline – because it's hers to control. We are not saying don't love your wife and we are not saying don't shower her with affection. All we are saying is to be aware of when your wife cannot take all your love and affection in and don't take it personally. Give her the space to go through the emotions she needs to go through, so that she can arrive in a place where she can receive all that you have to give – in most cases, it has nothing to do with you but more with what is going on for her. Be of service to her.

48
MY WIFE IS MY BEST FRIEND... BULLSH*T!

My wife is my best friend."

When a husband says the above statement, red flags go up right away. This statement alone reveals so much about where a husband is at – not only in his relationship, but also his whole life.

From the relationship perspective, this highlights a very high level of unhealthy codependency in the marriage. We are using the word "codependency" because it is most likely a two-way street. The husband has a high degree of unhealthy dependency on the wife (with a special focus on emotional dependency) and the wife also has a high degree of unhealthy dependency (with a special focus on her self-image). The two mutual dependencies create what we call codependency. To further understand the negative impact of dependency, let's differentiate between the words "want" and "need" through everyday life examples so that you can clearly translate it into the relationship context.

"I want alcohol tonight," says the man who wants to go out and have a fun time. "I need alcohol tonight," says the alcoholic. "I want a piece of pie after dinner," says the woman who is choosing to enjoy a nice post-dinner sweet. "I need a piece of pie after dinner," says the sugar addict. "I want to go to the casino and test my luck," says the risk-tolerant person wanting to spice things up in his everyday life. "I need to go to the casino and win my losses back," says the gambling addict.

I believe you see the point being made here. When you apply these everyday examples of wants vs. needs to a relationship that has a high degree of codependency, you can quickly differentiate what the wants and what the needs are in the marriage. In a highly codependent marriage, the needs significantly outweigh the wants. Need for approval, need for appreciation, need for respect, need to acknowledgement, need for being right and the list goes on.

This takes place because of the need to rely on his spouse is mutual to the degree that the husband's identity becomes threatened without his spouse. Ideas of self-sufficiency quickly evaporate, and they do so quietly in the background over the years that pass by.

From the masculinity perspective, when the husband says, "My wife is my best friend," it clearly indicates that authentic, vulnerable masculine relationships are non-existent for him. The husband most likely has zero men in his life who keep him accountable, who call him on his bullshit and to whom he can feel safe to expose himself to without feeling judged. In turn, he now relies on his wife – who is dominated by the feminine – to fill that void. The fact of the matter is that the feminine is not the masculine. The characteristics of these two are different, often polar opposites, which is why traditional men and women attract each other. This can also be true for non-heterosexual couples, as usually one is significantly more feminine while the other more masculine, irrelevant of gender.

Now, let's look at the statement "My wife is my best friend" from the perspective of terms and purpose. A husband for whom the above two points around relationship and masculinity are in place will very likely compromise himself as a man, which will cause him to pretend to be somebody he is not. He will give in on aspects of his life to please his wife because the need to be liked and approved of overtakes him. Similarly, a husband will compromise his purpose – if he even has one outside of marriage – for the same reasons. Eventually, his purpose becomes his wife, which in later years deepens his codependency and suffocates her. Purpose must be additional to family so that he can reliably boost his self-confidence and self-worth.

Lastly, let's look at the same statement from a perspective of decision-making and being the "bowl" in the marriage. The feminine requires a safe space to ensure that emotional needs are met. When a husband is codependent and becomes equally emotional and shares his emotions to the degree that it overtakes the safe space for her to share hers, it will cause the wife to eventually shut down because she now has to manage and babysit the husband's emotions. She will think he cannot handle her by being the "bowl," by being the rock. Hence, her nurturing mechanism kicks in, which over time turns into a lack of attraction, suffocation and an over-compensating, masculine wife. This will lead to her wanting out of the marriage long-term.

With all the above explained, we are not saying your wife cannot be your friend. In fact, she *should* be your friend. A close one too. It is foundational to have mutual trust. What we are saying is that the masculine and feminine have their own needs that need to be met by the same side. The masculine leans on the masculine for certain aspects of life and the feminine leans on the feminine for certain aspects of life. Having said that, the solution to this generational problem of "My wife is my best friend" is actually quite simple: build authentic and vulnerable masculine relationships in your life. A tribe of men who don't judge you and always have your back. That is exactly what The Bulletproof Husband does and gives each and every day to its members.

Warning: your wife will always try to make you her best friend. Do not blame her for it. She manages the relationship and has the skill set for it. It is your job to draw the line in a masculine way as described above.

49
BOUNDARIES ARE FOR GIRLS (MEN HAVE TERMS)

There are countless books, podcasts, and online videos about creating boundaries and I want to warn you: as a man, don't fall into this trap.

The metaphor goes that when something is valuable, it needs boundaries, since that's why bank vaults have walls (so far, so good). As a solid, masculine man, your terms are your only boundaries. Once you are clear on your terms, you don't need any other boundaries. "But what if my wife is screaming at me, being disrespectful, swearing at me etc.?" Then she is feeling safe enough to splash and trusting you to help her get the venom out – that's awesome! Why would you ruin that by throwing up a boundary? "Listen babe, I don't want to be yelled at. How about you come back when you are capable of having a respectful conversation and we can continue?"

I've been there and done that, and it is extremely unproductive and unmasculine. If you do that, you are grabbing the management of the relationship, which is a very controlling and untrusting thing to do. And the only reason you'd do such a thing is because you can't handle what she is saying, which means your bullet is being poked. If you can't handle what she is saying, use an exit strategy, get out of there, and go responsibly pull out your bullet, then get back to her so she can finish letting the venom out.

If you are still requiring her to be "respectful," then you have missed many of the major components in being a masculine man. Once you become emotionally self-sufficient and don't need or require her respect, because you have overflowing levels of respect for yourself, then if she treats you respectfully, it is simply a bonus win. Unfortunately, there is a current phenomenon on social media where "players" and other "pseudo-alphas" are saying that if you aren't being respected, then cut her out of your life. This is the other side of the toxic masculinity coin: insecure beta-males and insecure pseudo-alphas. The truly secure masculine man has no need to run away from someone being disrespectful, manipulative etc., unless it would cause him to violate his terms.

So are we enabling women? Let's say for example that your wife has an addiction issue and is endangering the children. In that case, you would be violating your terms if you didn't protect your children – therefore, you would set a boundary. When something is going to cause you to violate your terms, set boundaries. Terms determine the how and when of not enabling.

I have a personal example of when I had to set very strong boundaries around my terms back in 2020. It was when my extended family admitted in court that they were the ones calling in false reports to Child Protective Services about my wife and me. At that point, we decided to go no-contact with them and my term of being a "man who provides safety and love for my family" needed to been protected. I chose to not enable them in their delusions and mental illness, which was endangering my family.

Remember the hierarchy of decision-making: your terms, her

management of the relationship, your purpose, your feelings and wants. As a masculine man, you only need to set boundaries to protect your terms – you should trust her management of the relationship, and regarding your purpose and especially your feelings and wants, you don't need to apply boundaries. There is no clearer picture of the insecure beta-male than one who is trying to protect his feelings from being hurt by the mean, scary world and feminine energy. In the immortal words of the country singer Leigh Guest: "Fuck your feelings."

On the flipside, the feminine woman is guided by her feelings. As a master of managing relationships, she will set boundaries a thousand times more than any masculine man. She will set boundaries to manage the relationship, to test you, to give you an opportunity to rebuild trust, and to help her feel safe when you are still being an asshole. Boundaries are a mainstay for women. The bottom line is that the masculine and feminine are extremely different and if that "unfairness" still bothers you, then it is poking your bullet and you should deal with it.

Once anyone, anywhere can say anything to you and you are able to remain solid, consistent and reliably the bowl for them, you will know that you are being an eight-foot-tall, barrel-chested, masculine man.

SECTION RECAP

- The sky is pink but it'll change: The conversation is rarely about finding agreement; it is about her feeling heard and understood.
- Her bullets come out verbally: The masculine must physically emote its feelings, whereas the feminine must verbally emote.
- But she's the one cheating! After you've starved her to death, you then blame her for finding crumbs to feed herself? Change your context, take responsibility.
- Vulnerability and intimacy: The wounds under your armor are the places where you are vulnerable. Share them with your tribe and do the work to heal them.
- Rejection gives her power: Deal with your inner little boy, so that you can have the confidence needed to be the man she can push away or pull in.
- Don't be a pleaser, don't be helpful, be of service: Stop playing the game of "giving to get." Give because that is who you are as a man.
- You are not responsible for her happiness: Your responsibility is to be a great husband. Her happiness and approval of you are bad goals that will keep you on a frustrating hamster wheel.
- Is she being masculine? If you are not going to step up

and provide masculinity, she will fill in the gap, but that is a heavy load for her to bear. Also it will set her up to be tempted by other men that are more masculine. Protect your family by being the most masculine one in the unit.

- You can't love her more than she loves herself: Pour your love into her and don't have expectations. She may or may not be able to receive what you are expressing to her. Express your love because that is who you are as a man.
- My wife is my best friend... Bullshit! The codependent and needy man is typically isolated from other men, has no masculine tribe and lives enmeshed in his martial relationship. This does not lead to a healthy polarity within the marriage.
- Boundaries are for girls: As a man, you only use boundaries when your terms are being endangered. As a man, feeling disrespected is not a valid reason to use boundaries.

MEMBER STORY: FROM FEMININE HUSBAND AND MASCULINE WIFE TO A FULL RECOVERY AND ROLE REVERSAL

I can clearly remember sitting down, alone, for the third night in a row in a dimly lit, run-down hotel room where I now lived. I was down nearly two bottles of my favorite red wine, and the foul smell of someone's cigarettes was wafting in the open window. With tears in my eyes and my heart hardened from anger, sorrow, hurt and resent, I sat there mindlessly scrolling through Facebook to distract myself from the painful thoughts of my recently deceased marriage.

A few days before, I had hastily packed my small gym bag with some toiletries and articles of clothing before storming out of the house and slamming the front door behind me. This cowardly act was the only way I could think of to avoid the inevitable recurring three-ring-shit-show-circus of an argument that was about to transpire for like the millionth time in my relationship. You see, there were never any big events like cheating, beating, bankruptcy or drugs. Instead, my insecurities, triggers, lack of confidence and lack of masculinity all added up over the years to slowly erode the already fragile foundation between us.

Obtusely oblivious to any of my own contribution to the downfall of my marriage, I was confused how I had wound up here, and how my beautiful wife, over the years, had turned cold, venomous and impossible to talk to. While absolutely hammered, in-between random movie fight scenes, science videos and stupid memes, I scrolled upon a random ad claiming it could teach me how to save my marriage. Figuring anything would be cheaper than the thousands we'd wasted on years of useless couple's counseling, I tapped the "learn more" button. Worth a shot, I guessed.

The free video intrigued me. I learned more about relation-ship dynamics in 45 minutes than I had in a lifetime from my parents, teachers and friends. The next day, for my breakthrough call, I connected with a jovial Irishman, whose accent I could barely understand, and whose approach I could only describe as a velvet hammer: concepts like 100% ownership, the water and the bowl, emotional midgets and giants and such, completely changed the way I looked at my frustrating life journey so far. Yes, I signed up on the spot! I couldn't believe such basic, fundamental life knowledge had somehow escaped me for over 40 years.

Within a matter of days, I was back in my home. Within a matter of weeks, my wife started to slowly and cautiously interact with me again. Within months, some amazing occasional intimacy started as I took the lead and pursued her again, and within a year, I can honestly say that from my hard work, the support of my tribe and the guidance of my coaches, my marriage is not only fully restored, but the bond, connection and understanding we have between us is much closer than it has ever been. This whole time, my wife has been almost as surprised as me at the total absence of any of our familiar blow-ups or arguments.

My journey in becoming the man, husband and father I've always wanted to be will never be complete, but looking back, I know one night that I, at least, achieved a certain level, when my wife and I were laughing and dancing bachata in the kitchen, in our pajamas, just after the little one had been put to bed and the teenagers had finally stopped eating to get back to their video games. She looked at me sweetly as I led her across the smooth tile floor and said she appreciated all the hard work I did, and she had seen that potential in me all along.

I owe my marriage and my masculinity to the amazing men I've met, and their lessons, on this journey from insecure, lonely rundown hotel room resident to the proud, confident leader of my household that I am becoming.

UNDERSTANDING TRUST

50
TRUST DYNAMICS

There are countless perspectives on the topic of trust and trust-building. From what I have seen, I have found The Bulletproof Husband to have a profoundly unique understanding of trust.

Let's say for example that when you first came across The Bulletproof Husband philosophy, you were a highly insecure and easily triggered man. After figuring out your terms, letting your wife manage the relationship, connecting with some tribesmen, and pulling out some deep bullets, you are now able to consistently show up for her as the bowl and you are not triggerable. This is huge progress and we see this happen consistently in our membership. At this point, she now trusts you to not get triggered. You could easily stop here and you would be a much better man than you used to be. Yet if you really want to be the man you've always wanted to be, the type of man you'd want your son to be when he grows up, as well as the type of man you'd want your daughter to marry, then you need to go further. It isn't enough to simply be the bowl for the feminine splashing. In some ways, that can end up being very passive and it doesn't build trust into other parts of the relationship.

When you use TBH tools, doing things like Spot Apologies, it builds her trust in your ability to take 100% responsibility. When you build masculine relationships and have accountability, it builds her trust that you are emotionally self-sufficient and won't be needy and codependent on her. When you use HUAV and OEQs in listening to her, it builds her trust that you will empathetically care for her. When you do the Full BPAs, it builds her trust in your emotional work and the deep changes that have taken place in you.

Each of these tools will build trust in a different way and each time you build trust, you are making a deposit into the relationship. At The Bulletproof Husband, we think of trust as a currency in the emotional realm. It helps to think of the relationship like a bank account that you can make deposits into, where some actions can cause withdrawals. Most men seek out TBH once they have already overdrafted the emotional trust in the relationship by about a million dollars and everything is teetering on the edge of divorce (the relationship equivalent of a trust bankruptcy, including a repossession – i.e. the slap). The tools of TBH help you establish a new relationship with your wife (the trust bank account manager) and help you make consistent, steady deposits which pay back your indebtedness and get you out of the red and back into the black.

As the trust bank account manager, she is deeply aware of all your deposits and withdrawals. She keeps track of them in a mental relationship bankbook. If you had an affair, that would be a huge withdrawal of trust from the bank account. It would take hundreds of consistent deposits over time (typically five to ten years) for that withdrawal to get knocked off the bankbook.

Some withdrawals are intentional and not damaging to the relationship – for example, when my wife trusted me enough to move our family 800 miles away to a new hometown. This required a lot of trust and was a huge withdrawal. Yet over time, the trust was redeposited and actually multiplied because the move proved to be such a positive choice for our family.

The most important point here is becoming aware of trust as a currency and intentionally making deposits to rebuild the trust account. If you have gotten the slap, you have a lot of trust to rebuild before you reach the end of Stage Two. If you get to the beginning of Stage Three, you are starting with a zero balance. You are out of debt, but you don't have any leeway to be making withdrawals yet. The beginning of Stage Three means that your relationship is similar to you walking up to a girl in a bar and beginning to hit on her. She may be interested but she doesn't have any reason to trust you yet. Your trust level with her is at zero and you will have to build from there.

Lastly, when you are proactively building trust, you are demonstrating leadership (which is incredibly attractive). The reverse is also true: if someone doesn't trust you, then you can't lead them anywhere. So I will say it again: if you use the tools of this program, you will build her trust and she will be the manager of the relationship, but you will be the leader of the relationship again.

51
TRUSTING MAKES YOU A LEADER

When you trust someone with something, it draws it out in them. Let's say for example that you raise a toast in honor of your friend at a party. You say, "He is one of my oldest friends; he has been faithful through thick and thin; I trust him with my life, my wife and my life savings. He is an honorable man and there are few like him." For the rest of that night, your friend is going to walk, speak, stand and interact with people in a different way. That kind of trust and honor actually draws something out in the person on the receiving end.

For you to give trust like that is a form of leadership. You are showing people how to treat your friend and you are drawing something out in your friend. He actually becomes more trustworthy because of your trusting leadership. Also when you are giving trust, you are demonstrating confidence and are very attractive.

Typically, trust is uncommon, and people hold back on giving trust because of the risk of getting hurt, especially when the trust is unearned. However, if you are going to be 100% responsible in your life and 0% a victim, then you will find that you can trust others because you are choosing to take ownership for both your actions and the actions of the person you are trusting.

When you give trust to another person, you are giving a gift that demonstrates that you love them. This is powerful in rebuilding your marriage, especially when you are scared of how she is going to manage the relationship. Yet if you give trust, you are communicating a rare form of love. Also, when you demonstrate trust, you will be leading her toward trusting you as well. When it comes to trust, what you sow is what you reap.

Another definition of trust is a firm belief in them having three qualities:

- Honesty
- Integrity
- Reliability

Having trust in all three components is powerful, especially when there is a proper balance of the three. Perhaps someone is honest with you, but maybe they don't have integrity. Not having integrity means you might be stabbed in the back by their character and choices. Someone else might be completely honest and integrous, yet unreliable because they have not put accountability structures in their life. This type of person will continually drain your trust because they have nothing in place in their life to keep them consistent and reliable. To trust someone fully is to believe in their ability to provide all three components.

52
THE GIFT OF TRUSTING

Trusting comes with a cost. When you trust someone, you are opening yourself up to getting new bullets. The most important thing is to be proactive, so that when you get hurt, you pull the bullet and get right back to trusting.

There are three main ways that she will do things that hurt you and make you not want to trust her:

1. Dishonesty: Dishonesty is pretty self-explanatory. If she lies to you, it is easy to feel hurt and devalued. Once you release the emotional pain and get your head on straight, you will need to take full responsibility for being lied to. Why would she lie? Because she doesn't feel safe to tell the truth. How have you not made her feel safe? How can you make her feel safe enough to tell the truth in the future?

2. Unreliability: This is a little different. If your wife is constantly late, you will need raise the trust level high enough in the relationship so that she will follow your leadership. Also when she fails to be on time, you will need to take the ownership of where you lacked the trust and leadership ability to lead her. The challenge with unreliability is that your ego wants to take it personally and feel disrespected. Do the emotional work to deal with those feelings and get back to trusting and leading.

3. An integrity and values mismatch: This is the most challenging obstacle to trusting. When you find out she is cheating on you, it takes a brutal emotional toll. You will need to grieve the loss of your old relationship and pull out the feelings of betrayal. Once you have gotten to the bottom of those feelings, you will need to take 100% ownership again. A powerfully responsible man is able to see that he likely failed to love, honor and cherish his wife adequately, which left her open to an affair by being led in the direction of having her feelings cared for. A new context for a responsible man to carry is that he is working on becoming the kind of husband she would be a fool to leave.

At the end of the day, even if your wife leaves you, she is still your co-parent in a partnership for the kids. You will still need to establish a trusting relationship for the sake of the kids.

HELPFUL TIPS FOR GIVING THE GIFT OF TRUST

1. Do not take a woman at her word. The saying is "Be a man of your word," not "Be a woman of your word." She will change her mind based on her feelings. For her to be in integrity means that she is being authentic and honoring her feelings in the moment. In one moment she will say, "I hate you; I never want to be with you," and five minutes later she will say, "Let's get dressed up and go out to dinner tonight." To a man, this sounds bi-polar. To a woman, this is the feminine following her feelings. To a man, this sounds like she is being dishonest, but to the feminine, this is 100% honest because she is telling the truth in the moment that she is feeling it. It is completely true in the moment it comes out of her lips, yet it can change in the next moment. Also the feminine sometimes simply has to say it out loud to kind of "try it on and see if that is how I actually feel," although she isn't going to tell you that she is test-driving her own feelings.

2. It's not necessarily a payable debt. When you are choosing to give trust, it is like giving a loan without interest and without obligation to pay it back. If they waste the loan, don't take it as them betraying your trust.

3. Don't trust her with your terms. You must handle your terms yourself. For example, I have a term about keeping my family safe. Part of how this applies is that at the end of the night, I lock all the doors of my house. Even if my wife says she has locked the doors, I will double-check each lock before I go to sleep. I do that because it is my term and I am responsible for that. I make sure that I silently check and I don't mention what I am doing. This keeps my wife feeling trusted, but I am making sure that my terms are not being compromised.

4. Always trust in her management of the relationship. This is the most important area in which to trust her and sometimes the hardest, especially when she is managing the relationship into divorce or into affairs, etc. This is the most powerful area in which to keep choosing to trust.

5. The decision to trust is a choice. Trust isn't a logical choice. It is a masculine choice. Trust is an extension of who you are as a man. Trust is often not a smart thing to do, and you will have to accept that trusting is naïve and can look stupid to others.

Let's say that you're a masculine man who has chosen to be responsible and to trust his wife. One day you come home and find your wife naked in your bed with another man. Your first thought as a trusting man would be, "He must have hypothermia and she is trying to save his life!" Yeah. I know. That sounds INSANE. Yet there is a one-in-a-billion chance that you could be right. The most powerful choice you can make in the face of that situation would be to land on the naïve trusting side.

Being this level of trusting will include you having to stab your own ego, but in the longer term, this level of trusting can help you lead the relationship to a new place. It demonstrates your solidness.

When she does something shitty, you will feel your trust get stabbed. You will need to do the emotional work, pull out the bullet and choose to trust her fully again. Don't become an untrusting person – that is guaranteed to erode the relationship and you will be giving up your solidness and leadership.

The bottom line is this: if you aren't trusting her, that is because of your bullets. Always.

6. Remember, trust is not a trade. "I trust her and I expect her to trust me" – no. You give trust unconditionally, whereas you have to earn her trust. Trust isn't about fairness. Trust is a powerful leadership tool. Your responsibility is to trust her 100% unconditionally and be responsible to earn trust. And when you are giving trust as a gift, it can't be violated.

53
TRUSTING WITH ZERO EXPECTATIONS

The degree to which you trust your wife is a direct reflection of your own security as a man and your clarity of role as a husband.

If you cannot trust your wife fully, without any additional expectations, that says something about you as a man. There is some sort of insecurity that does not allow you to trust her. It could be because she cheated on you, or something like how she is always late or loses her keys. Whatever you are not trusting her with, that tells a story about your insecurities as a man.

Your role as a man and husband is to trust your wife unconditionally. As contradictory as it sounds, trust from a husband toward a wife is a must, whereas trust from a wife toward a husband must be earned. Your trust as a man is a choice and it is given as a gift without expectations.

GUIDING POINTS ON TRUSTING WITHOUT EXPECTATIONS
1. It must be your choice. If your trust is based on your feelings

and not a choice, she will be in control of your trust. This actually makes you weak and controllable. She will feel that and know that you are not solid, you are triggerable, you are not responsible and you are unsafe. This will set you up for brutal testing from her and makes you very unattractive.

2. It must be unconditional. If you don't trust her unconditionally, you are going to be disappointed and hurt. This will give you new bullets. Whenever you feel like someone "betrayed your trust," you are telling the story of how you gave yourself a new bullet by having expectations and didn't unconditionally trust.

3. It must be independent of the other person's response. If you keep giving trust and then keep feeling violated, your motivation will eventually fail. You will eventually throw in the towel and say it is too painful to trust again. However, if you choose to give trust as a gift, then it doesn't matter what the other person does with the gift.

4. Nobody else is responsible for your trust. If you choose to be 100% responsible, to choose to give trust without expectations and to operate from confidence, you will feel solid and masculine. If you choose to base your trust on her actions and whether that makes you feel like trusting or not, you will regularly feel insecure and emasculated as a man. You will be relying on her to make you feel safe.

5. Doing it right will make you grow. If you choose to take responsibility and give trust unconditionally without expectations, you will experience something that very few men get to experience: the giving of an extraordinary masculine gift. It is an extremely rare man who can keep giving trust in the face of what would crumble other men. Self-protecting men would call it foolish, wasteful or naïve, yet it is one of the highest forms of leadership. To keep choosing to give trust is to be the metaphorical eight-foot-tall, barrel-chested man. That level of trust will let her flourish and help break her out of destructive patterns. It makes her feminine and makes you more attractive.

54
TRUST ACCOUNT

As a masculine man, you are 100% responsible for trusting her, whether she has earned it or not, yet this is a double-edged sword because you are also responsible for gaining her trust conditionally. The positive side of this is that you can always see where you stand in the relationship because the trust level will be like the indicator lights on your dashboard. One of the biggest clues is that the more she trusts you, the less she tests you.

Whether you think you have broken her trust or not, if the relationship has been slapped, you are going to need to rebuild and regain her trust. Even if she is the one out there cheating, at some point you have lost her trust and are no longer able to lead her back until you rebuild that trust.

THERE ARE DIFFERENT TYPES OF DEPOSITS

1. You demonstrate honesty, integrity or reliability.
2. You show that you have her best interests at heart.
3. You make her feel taken care of. Women equate that to love, like men equate acceptance to love.
4. You make her feel good about herself. Men naturally have larger egos (imagine the ego that it must take to

attack a saber-tooth tiger!), whereas women typically have a smaller ego, which is helpful for connections and relationships with others in the tribe. One of the most attractive things a man can do with his big ego is boost a woman's ego and help her feel good about herself (if you're aiming to not have affairs, be careful with this superpower that you have).

5. You make her feel heard, understood, appreciated and valued.
6. She feels that she got her way (e.g. if there is a disagreement and you let her have it her way).

THE FLIPSIDE OF WITHDRAWALS

1. A lack of honesty is a big withdrawal.
2. A lack of integrity means you are triggerable, not safe and not changing.
3. A lack of reliability (e.g. you don't keep your promises) is a withdrawal.
4. Any unfavorable surprises without warning (e.g. "Hey honey, the in-laws are coming over tonight") is a withdrawal.
5. If she feels forced to give in and you are just getting your way, that is a withdrawal.
6. Any time she feels unsafe, you get angry, yell, you jab at one of her deep hurts (e.g. "I knew you were broken because your dad left you") is a big withdrawal.

TIPS ON MANAGING THE BALANCE

1. If you are making requests with a zero or negative balance, they will likely be rejected.
2. When the balance is high, you will typically get a yes.

3. Some withdrawals are an investment into you, and
    you are then able to redeposit them as an increase (e.g.
    "Let's move back in together," or "Let's do a family vaca-
    tion." If these go well, it turns into a great deposit!).

4. How will you know the amount of trust in your account?
    The most obvious way of measuring trust is how much
    she vulnerably shares with you. When you meet the
    average stranger, they don't share vulnerably until a
    measure of trust is built up with you. The same with
    your wife. Since you are starting with a deficit, you have
    to get back to the end of Stage Two to get to the stranger
    level. Then, you have to build from there before she
    really even begins to share vulnerably with you. If you
    were to walk up to the hot chick at the bar and start
    chatting her up, you would be beginning at the start of
    Stage Three. If you are going to build a new relationship
    with your wife, you will have to do all the trust rebuild-
    ing to get back to the starting point of Stage three.

55
RELATIONSHIP BANKBOOK

The relationship bankbook is a listing of trust account highlights: the big deposits and big withdrawals. It helps her understand why she does or doesn't trust you. Big items stay in the bankbook for a long time, medium items for lesser time and small deposits and withdrawals drop off quickly.

At any time, there is a finite list of items that can fit on the bankbook list. The older, really big deposits and withdrawals will be on the list, as well as the newer and smaller withdrawals and deposits. A large withdrawal such as you having cheated on her 10 years ago – she will remember that. You having given her a cup of coffee this morning – she will forget that by tomorrow.

The finite list is based on the idea that she can only remember so many things, so she has to be selective with her memory. This can actually work in your favor though because the more deposits you make, it will eventually bump off the withdrawals.

Once you begin to proactively change the balance in the bankbook, it will change how she sees you and the relationship. Let's look closer at what happens when she pulls out the bankbook.

The bankbook comes out when she is upset. That is when she starts reviewing all the withdrawals to justify to herself why she is upset.

Another time she will pull out the bankbook is when she thinks your ego is too big. She will then manage your ego by listing out your withdrawals. Also, when you make a withdrawal from the account, the bankbook will come out and she will review past times that you made a withdrawal, especially similar withdrawals.

There are a couple positive times that the book comes out as well. When you are feeling down, she will list out some of your deposits in the trust account. This is a part of her management of your ego. If your ego is too big, she will bring up your withdrawals, but if you are feeling low, she will bring up deposits such as, "You are a really good man; remember when you..."

If your ego is too big or too small, both fall into the realm of unsafe for her. And what's big and small is relative to your integrity and accountability. If you are managing a company of 10 employees and you are braggadociously saying that you could easily manage a company of 1,000 employees, she is going to bring you down before you do something stupid. If you manage a company of 900 employees and say that you are going to grow to 1,000 employees, then your ego is probably not scaring her and making her feel unsafe.

The time when the most complete listing of your deposits comes out will be in her eulogy at your funeral.

MAKE ROOM FOR THE BOOK

Don't be triggered by or argue with the withdrawals. You took the withdrawals and you have to proactively build the trust back until it knocks the withdrawal off the record.

Don't create your own bankbook or keep track of her deposits and withdrawals. The masculine chooses to trust unconditionally – this is how you lead the relationship. When you take on 100% responsibility in the relationship, she can't make a withdrawal because whatever she does is really "your" doing. If you start keeping track of her withdrawals, you are stepping into blame and not being responsible as the leader.

Having a bankbook is a feminine way of managing the feelings of safety. If a man is keeping a bankbook, he is acting in a feminine way. The feminine bases trust on feelings and past actions, whereas the masculine bases trust on self-trust. The masculine chooses to trust because he trusts himself and his ability to be responsible and lead no matter what happens. If you are feeling your own bankbook building against her, you must step back into taking responsibility for what you have been blaming her for, and responsibly let out the suppressed feelings you have built up. Then get back to trusting her unconditionally.

56
UNSPOKEN
PROMISES

A *spoken* promise is where the chapter "Your Word Is Your Bond, Part 2" comes into the marriage relationship.

Each time you give your word and then keep your spoken promise, the value of your word increases. The trust that you are a man of your word increases. It helps to start with being impeccable with your time management and your current commitments. If something is scheduled, be on time. If you have already committed to doing something around the house, get it done without her ever mentioning it; simply own it.

The opposite is an *unspoken* promise. The unspoken promise can be tricky to notice and for most men, it is a trap that we fall into. Let's say for example that you start helping around the house more frequently and you take the garbage to the curb each week for four weeks in a row. Your wife will be upset with you if you don't remember to take it to the curb on the fifth week. You may try to defend yourself and argue that you never committed to take it out every week, but your consistently habitual actions spoke louder than words and you ended up making an unspoken promise. Watch out for creating unspoken promises because they create a lot of arguments in marriage; instead, only consciously take on responsibilities and communicate about them clearly.

SECTION RECAP

- Trust dynamics: Trust is like a currency and you have to learn how to be aware of it and manage it.
- Trusting makes you a leader: When you are trusting, you are going to pull the best out of those you are trusting.
- The gift of trusting: Trust is a choice you make; it is not a feeling and it is not led by your feelings.
- Trusting with zero expectations: Trust cannot be betrayed; it is a gift you gave away and others can value it or not.
- The trust account: With trust being a currency, you can know if you are overdrafting your relationship bank account or if you are making deposits. Be aware of the balance and be intentional.
- The relationship bankbook: Your woman will keep a log of trust-building and trust-depleting actions you have taken. You can intentionally add to or subtract from your trust bank account.
- Unspoken promises: When you do something repeatedly, expectations are formed. Even if you did not explicitly give your word, your wife will start to expect you to keep doing certain things. Be aware of these unspoken promises.

MEMBER STORY: FROM SMASHING DISHES TO TRUST COMPLETELY REBUILT

Only a couple months ago, my wife and I stood in the dimly lit kitchen, the stars shining brightly through the open sliding glass door. We were embracing each other as tears rolled down her cheeks after she'd just shared some of her deep hurts from the past. I could feel her heart open to me as I looked deep in her eyes and then kissed her forehead.

It wasn't always like this. Months prior to this, I was trying desperately to keep myself together in the face of her emotions, her complaints. I was always taking it personally, always blaming her back, with resentment, even smashing the coffee mug on the ground in front of her in the garage in anger. Why couldn't I be the man that could bear her pleas, or allow myself to listen to her heartbreak? This had gone on for years. In an attempt to end the cloud of misery we both lived in, she told me to not come home until I found my own place. This was all I could take, at this point, I cracked. I ran out of the house crying uncontrollably, hopped in my truck and drove away.

It was on a long, lonely walk on the beach that day that I thought of my mentors who'd urged me to "Let go of the old resentment to begin the new relationship." In my desperation I decided to take full responsibility to be accountable to the men and mentors I was working with, and fully commit to myself, regardless of any relationship outcome… I needed to do this for me. This was the beginning of a journey into the depths of my soul to find my true potential. Men who'd succeeded before me laid it all out: all I had to do was the work to get past my fears and insecurities. Getting to the heart of my insecurities was an amazing discovery. Slowly, I noticed I was not reacting to her. Working on my insecurities wasn't easy, but eventually trust with my wife grew. She could trust me to listen to even the toughest things she had to say.

Standing here now, in front of the sliding glass door, embracing as she let out her tears, she drew in closer as I wrapped my arms around her. I knew I could hold all of it for her, in that space, in that moment, seeing her commitment behind what she'd expressed earlier. I'd finally arrived at a place where I could accept her, in all her forms and feelings. Be it anger or joy, happiness or sadness, this was the space I'd created. This was the space she'd always needed. And that is why I am talking to you today.

TAKING OWNERSHIP

57
DRAWING A LINE IN THE SAND

The purpose of the Mini-BPA is to ask for more time from your wife and to let her know you're becoming self-aware and intend to work on yourself. Yet as you will see, you are not directly asking her for more time. Rather, you are letting her know that if she waits, she will see you working on yourself and it will be worth the wait.

You will only give her the Mini-BPA one time, and it essentially draws a line in the sand between the old relationship that is being left behind and the new relationship that can be built as you become a new man.

THERE ARE FOUR MAIN COMPONENTS TO THE MINI.

STEP 1: BEGIN BY THANKING YOUR WIFE FOR GIVING YOU THE SLAP AND WAKING YOU UP.

This letter is one-sided and entirely focused on you and what you are going to work on in yourself. You won't be mentioning anything about what the relationship needs or what she should be working on; this is about you and how you are thankful that she woke you up. This first section looks like this:

Thank you. Thank you for waking me up. Thank
you for turning my world upside down because you
have opened my eyes. I see this whole new world of
developing myself that I hadn't seen before. Thank
you for letting me see what an asshole I have been
to you in our marriage/relationship. Thank you for
taking the actions you needed to take to bring me
to this place of awareness about myself. I could not
have done this without you.

The fact of the matter is that as soon as she hears you say that you have been an asshole, her ears will perk up and you will have her full attention, especially if you don't typically swear.

STEP 2: STATE YOUR INTENTION TO WORK ON YOURSELF.

She has probably been feeling blamed and attacked by you in recent arguments, so the Mini sets a whole new tone to the relationship. It lets her know that you are seeing the problems and taking owner-ship. That she doesn't have to carry you anymore and can let you go work on yourself. Here's what Step 2 looks like:

You [wanting to separate/divorce, telling me you
love me but are not in love with me, cheating on me
(personalize this sentence to your situation)] has
opened the door to seeing myself in a way I have
not seen myself before. Because you opened my
eyes, I see there is a whole new realm for develop-
ing myself, which I wasn't aware of before. In that
realm, I can see that a lot of growth is needed and
there is a ton of work for me to do before I can actu-
ally give you what you need in this relationship. I
can't really tell you what that work is yet. I am in
that discovery process but I can see a bunch of stuff
already [list one to three behaviors that you can see

that you need to start working on: I have been con-trolling, manipulative, unfaithful, verbally abusive, an addict etc. Let her know that you are beginning to work on these issues and MAKE NO PROMISES HERE; just inform her you are starting to work on these].

STEP 3: GIVE HER FREEDOM.

If she feels like you are doing this to win her back, then she will push back against it. So in Step 3, you are letting her know that you are doing this work to become the man you have always wanted to be, and you are doing the work for yourself. Also it moves the relationship toward Stage One by entrusting her to manage the relationship and by giving up all control. This section looks like so:

I have started on this journey to better myself as a man, husband and father. I will continue this journey of growth because I see that I need to change. I know that this transformation must be done by me irrespective of what decisions you make about our relationship. And I fully trust that you will do what's best for us and our family – whether it is keeping it together or not.

STEP 4: ASK FOR HELP AND TIME, WITHOUT ACTUALLY ASKING DIRECTLY.

By asking her to observe and watch you, you are being humble, and it lets her know that you are not expecting her involvement other than to simply watch you like a hawk, which she will likely be doing anyway. Here's Step 4:

I do need to ask for your help in all of this, though. This journey is a four-month program to really deal with these insecurities to the point where I can promise you that you will be able to look at me and things will be different. I can't do that just yet. I see an aspect of how I can make these changes permanent and I am starting that work. I am going to need your help to make sure I am on track. I need your help to watch me. To see if it's really going on track, I'll talk to you about it and ask you about it along the way. And once I do something that is permanent, I will come back and tell you about it. Thank you once again for waking me up and opening my eyes.

You may be wondering why it says "four months" in Step 4? We have found that after decades of being an asshole, foundational change typically takes a minimum of four months of: diligently doing the emotional work to pull bullets, keeping a wins journal, forging strong masculine accountability relationships, and being challenged by your Bulletproof Husband tribesmen to really make the deep and lasting change your wife and kids need from you. As discussed in a previous chapter ("Lone Wolves Get Slaughtered"), you aren't going to be able to implement all the tools and changes in this book all by yourself. Men do their best work on themselves when they are within a masculine community. That's why it is important to join The Bulletproof Husband online membership if you haven't already.

IN SUMMARY

Use the script provided. Only personalize the section regarding your specific behaviors. Don't make this letter any longer than provided. Typically, men with the Stupid bullet try to nitpick the Mini. Trust me: do it the way it is provided. One of the top complaints is, "This doesn't sound like me..." Yeah, I know. But what you have been doing isn't working. So it's time to try something new and this has been specifically crafted for your benefit and has been used by thousands of men so far.

Also don't delay: give the Mini as soon as possible. Lastly, it doesn't matter what her response is. She could interrupt you and start screaming at you and storm out, she could glare and listen and say nothing, she could melt and cry and swoon into your arms and asking you to make passionate love to her (although not bloody likely!). None of that matters. Just draw the line in the sand between the old and new relationship by delivering the Mini, then get to work on yourself.

Warning: Don't give the mini-BPA if you haven't yet joined The Bulletproof Husband program, otherwise you aren't going to be able to follow through on making the changes you committed to making.

For more info about joining go to
www.BulletproofHusband.com/DocJon

58
YOU'RE ON FIRE! STOP, DROP AND ROLL

After you have delivered the Mini-BPA, you will be focused on pulling bullets and working on yourself over the next four months. Inevitably, during this time, you will make mistakes and fail at times. You might forget to take care of something you promised your wife, or you might get triggered and snap at her. This is where the Spot Apology comes into play.

The Spot Apology is short and super-direct. It can be said verbally, which is the best-case scenario, but it can also be texted to her and that is almost as good. The reason it is called a "Spot Apology" is because you want to deliver it right away – as in "on the spot." Typically try to give your Spot Apologies as soon as possible, the sooner the better.

A SPOT APOLOGY HAS FIVE COMPONENTS:

1. Acknowledge that you did something wrong. No

defending, explaining, etc. Just straight up say that she was right.

2. Communicate that you are not clear about why you did what you did. Be honest and simply say, "I reacted," or "I was triggered," "... and I don't know why," etc.

3. Communicate that you will look into the source of where that behavior came from.

4. Communicate that you will come back and let her know when you have dealt with it permanently. By saying this, you are setting yourself up for the time when you will come back and give her a Full Bulletproof Apology regarding this behavior.

5. Thank her for helping you see that behavior in yourself. This step actually builds her up and keeps you from sounding like a defensive victim.

The power of a Spot Apology is that it shows her that you are growing in your self-awareness and in your ability to take responsibility when you screw up. Giving a Spot Apology actually takes what was a removal of trust and turns it into a deposit of trust in the relationship. Also be sure to keep track of your Spot Apologies because you have just given your word as a man and your integrity is at stake if you don't come back to explain where this behavior came from in a Full BPA.

You will see in the sample Spot Apology below that we never include the word "sorry" in Bulletproof Apologies. Why not? Well, she has heard "sorry" from you for a long time and she is sick to death of hearing it. Don't even bother putting it in at this point in the relationship. Let your ownership of the situation communicate that you are sorry. Also don't use a Spot Apology to calm her down. Only give a Spot Apology if you actually see that you did something wrong or something you are not proud of. This isn't a tool to get her to stop being mad at you. Don't give her a Spot Apology to try to please her, and don't overuse these. Save them for the truly legitimate moments when it matters.

SAMPLE SPOT APOLOGY

[Her name], you are right. That was wrong of me. I am not sure why I did that. I will work on figuring out what the source of this behavior is. Once I figure it out and have permanently dealt with it, I will come back and let you know. Thank you for highlighting this for me.

59
ARE YOU READY TO BUILD MASSIVE TRUST?

At this point you have done the Mini-BPA, and maybe several Spot Apologies, as well as a lot of emotional work to pull out bullets. Once you have done enough bullet pulling to actually bring permanent changes to several behaviors, it is time to do a Full Bulletproof Apology. When you have crafted one of these masterpieces, you will find that in the letter, you will be taking on 100% responsibility for leading the relationship out of the ditch. Don't be the fool who waits for her to apologize; be the leader who demonstrates ownership and cleans up his own side of the street.

HERE ARE SOME OF THE MAJOR BENEFITS TO APOLOGIZING

- You bring the two of you into agreement. Yes, you were an asshole – you can both agree on that, and that is powerful.
- You are demonstrating masculine leadership by taking care of her hurt feelings.

- You are leading the way into ownership and might inspire her to apologize later.
- It gives her hope for a different husband, and that you are capable of changing.
- A proper apology helps her separate *you* from *your bullets* and helps her learn to blame your bullets. This helps her see that your hurts caused you to hurt her. When this is done well, it actually draws out her feminine-nurturer side and moves her out of feeling like a victim with you as the "bad guy."
- No matter how the other person responds, your self-respect and self-confidence will both increase when you clean up the messes you have made by taking ownership.

STRATEGIES FOR DELIVERING THE FULL BPA

1. **Be prepared.** Do all the emotional work you can so that you are calm, cool and collected.
2. **Be ready to listen away her emotions.** She is likely to get very emotional at some point in this process and that is a huge win! Be ready to help her get all those feelings out.
3. **Have thick armor.** This would be the worst time for you to get triggered and defensive. You MUST be ready for handling whatever she will say to you and remain the bowl.
4. **Go in 100% responsible.** If you are 99% responsible, then you are 1% a victim. Any victim mindset that is within you, she will sniff it out and jab at it. Make sure you deal with that and are showing up 100% responsible.
5. **Have an exit strategy.** The worst thing you can do is get argumentative in the middle of a Full BPA. Don't screw this up. Use an exit strategy and go to the bathroom for a few minutes if you are getting triggered.

6. **Be free of expectations.** It doesn't matter what she
   says or does in response. Once you drop a BPA, she
   will test you and once you pass the test, then her trust
   will grow. So in the meantime, don't be thrown by her
   response. Never expect anything in return from your
   wife. You will be disappointed most of the time if you do.
   Also, she measures your confidence level in what you do
   as a husband by the degree to which she feels you are
   expecting something in return. And if she sees expectation, she will leverage that against you. Or said another
   way, having no expectations of her means you will have
   a high level of confidence in her eyes, whereas you having expectations of her means you have a low level of
   confidence in her eyes.

7. **Be clear on what happens next.** Make sure you
   have a solid idea about cleaning up your messes and
   completing with yourself, regardless of how she takes
   your apology.

When you are done dropping a Full BPA, make sure you take a
few minutes to hoot and holler to celebrate the man you are being
and what you have just accomplished. You are being extremely rare
among men when you take this level of leadership and ownership.

60
SEVEN STEPS TO CLEANING UP YOUR PAST

Let's begin with a few important reminders: The apology is about the behavior, not the bullet. Each bullet has five to ten behaviors/ apologies. Be sure to spread out the apologies because each apology adds a deposit to the trust account – this means you shouldn't group a bunch of behaviors into one apology.

There are seven parts to giving a Full BPA. I will only skim over them below[17] and then I will tell you about my experience of sharing one of the BPAs when rebuilding trust with my wife.

17| My co-authors and I discussed at length whether or not to include an in-depth explanation of the Full BPAs and ultimately decided against it. This tool is very powerful and we concluded it would be like giving a shotgun to a three-year-old. It is absolutely essential that you have pulled out your bullets and put a tribe of masculine accountability relationships around yourself before you ever attempt giving a Full BPA. We can help you have everything you need within The Bulletproof Husband online program. Our perspective is captured by this quote: "An apology without changed behavior is simply manipulation."

1. Own the behavior
2. Own the root
3. Own the cost
4. Own the hurt
5. Own the work
6. Own the present
7. Own the future

The fifth BPA I gave my wife during our separation was about how I would get triggered, argue, and ruin holidays, vacations, birthdays, anniversaries and family time.

I vividly remember sitting on our couch as I shared this with her and when I asked her if there was more that she felt that I hadn't mentioned (one of the steps of the BPA), she unloaded for over an hour, recalling all the details and frustrations from over the years of ruined vacations and holidays. I listened carefully and patiently, and asked questions here and there to make sure she felt heard. To the untrained eye, it would seem that my apology wasn't being heard, that she was still just as mad as hell and didn't care what I had said. Yet the truth was that she was trusting me to help her get the pain out.

Once she got to the end of venting, I asked, "Is there anything else?" She said "No," so I thanked her for sharing that with me and if I could finish reading her the letter. She laughed and said she had forgotten entirely about the letter and yes, I should go ahead.

Once I had finished the letter, within a few hours, she invited me to go together on a family vacation for a week. Leading up to the vacation, she kept asking, "I know we are going for seven days – is that too long? Are you going to be able to handle that without getting stressed out?"

In the past, I would ruin most vacations that were longer than five days long because I would suppress my feelings for five days and then when I couldn't contain them anymore, I would explode. So I reassured her multiple times. By the end of the first week, she was shocked and actually extended the vacation by three extra days because she was having such a great time. Although we were still separated while on vacation and I slept in a different room during the trip, I passed the test and a huge deposit of emotional trust was put into my account.

When we arrived home, she shifted, ended the separation and invited me home from the place I was living. I was still in the guest room for another six weeks as trust continued to be restored, but this BPA and passing the test was a huge milestone. [18]

HERE IS THE ORDER OF THE JOURNEY I WALKED

- Joined TBH
- Delivered the Mini-BPA
- Delivered several Spot Apologies as needed
- Delivered Full BPAs:
    1. Manipulation and control
    2. Using people for my emotional needs
    3. Demanding respect and praise
    4. Blaming/projecting/stonewalling/defending
    5. Ruining vacations/holidays/anniversaries/birthdays
    6. Hiding things from her
    7. Being insecure about sex
    8. Being defensive and uncorrectable
    9. Putting my purpose above our marriage and family

I still use Spot Apologies when needed, and I have delivered many Full BPAs to other people. Most men need to deliver a minimum of six to ten BPAs to really take ownership of all the emotional

---

18| Note that there were multiple wins and tests here. 1) The pulling of my bullets that used to be triggered by special trips or events, 2) the pulling of bullets that made me capable of empathizing and hearing her vent without getting defensive, 3) the ability to cooperate with her management of the relationship from going on a trip together, to sleeping separately on the trip, to extending the trip, to inviting me home but only to the guest room at first, cooperated with her management all the way. Lastly, I will note again, BPAs should only be delivered when behavior has truly changed as the result of bullets being pulled.

damage they caused their wife over the years (although I do know men who have given over 20 Full BPAs!).

Although it can feel very intimidating to write and deliver these, the BPAs rebuild her trust in you and her emotional connection to you, and give her the ability to see a future together.[19]

19| One of the amazing resources within The Bulletproof Husband online membership are the coaches that can help you craft your BPAs.

61
APOLOGIES RESTORE TRUST WITH YOURSELF

The goal of all apologies in life is to restore your integrity with yourself. The other person may hold on to their hurt and blame you for the hurt, and that is their free-will choice. So keep your eyes on the real prize: being proud of who you are as a man. You are the kind of man who takes responsibility for your errors and does your best to clean up the mess. Each time you deliver a BPA, you are delivering a deposit in your own trust account and you will know yourself as a man worth trusting. When you reach the point where you have delivered all the BPAs you need to clean up the past and have owned your errors, you will feel "complete" with yourself. Each BPA delivered along the way is another step in the journey toward trusting yourself and feeling whole or complete.

Once you arrive at the point of having owned the past and all the bullets that used to drive you, you will be able to accept yourself fully and without hesitation.

AS "THE PROMISES" OF SEXAHOLICS ANONYMOUS STATES:

If we are painstaking about this phase of our development, we will be amazed before we are halfway through. We are going to know a new freedom and a new happiness. We will not regret the past nor wish to shut the door on it. We will comprehend the word serenity and we will know peace. No matter how far down the scale we have gone, we will see how our experience can benefit others. That feeling of uselessness and self-pity will disappear. We will lose interest in selfish things and gain interest in our fellows. Self-seeking will slip away. Our whole attitude and outlook upon life will change. Fear of people and of economic insecurity will leave us. We will intuitively know how to handle situations which used to baffle us. We will suddenly realize that God is doing for us what we could not do for ourselves.

Are these extravagant promises? We think not. They are being fulfilled among us sometimes quickly, sometimes slowly. They will always materialize if we work for them.

As you do the work of releasing BPAs, you will make progress with yourself. And if the person who receives the BPA chooses to release their pain and forgive you and form a new relationship with you, that is an external win. But the internal win comes the moment you deliver the BPA because you are being the kind of man you have always wanted to be. A solid man taking 100% responsibility for his life.

Warning: You must shift to doing apologies for yourself as a man. If you are apologizing to try to make someone happy with you again, you are approval seeking and controlled by external forces.

- Never apologize for anything unless you see that you weren't being the man you want to be.
- Never apologize to change the feelings of others, that is pure manipulation.
- Always apologize for acting from your bullets; because that isn't who you are, you were acting outside of your true self. You are not your bullets. If you pull out your bullets, your personality might even change. If you were laying in a hospital bed with nine bullet holes in you, it doesn't mean that you're not the kind of person that runs marathons; it means you can't currently run a marathon. Bullets change you in profound ways and make you seem like something you are not.

SECTION RECAP

- The Mini-Bulletproof Apology: This tool will help you draw a line in the sand between the old relationship and the new one you are beginning to build.
- The Spot Apology: With five simple components, you can take responsibility when you mess up and your woman won't feel like she has to push you to own your mistake.
- Preparing for the Full BPA: Giving a Full BPA is like running a marathon – it is something you must be trained and prepared for.
- The Full BPA: The Full BPA is a seven-step mega-tool for rebuilding trust in your relationship. You will need help crafting these.
- Completing with yourself: When you give a Full BPA, you are not only rebuilding trust with others, but you are also cleaning up the messy trail you left behind yourself and increasing your trust and self-respect.

MEMBER STORY: OWNING THE FAILURE AND CLEANING UP THE MESS

On a cool October morning in 2018, I woke at 4 am. Hunting season was here and the morning chill was perfect. Instead of getting up, I lay in bed reading men's Facebook posts in our private group. These men were trying to figure out how their relationship had got to such a dire place. My heart went out to them, because waking up alone every morning, without the woman I had vowed to love, honor, protect and cherish, was the pain I was dealing with daily.

How had I got here? What was my part in this? Why? WHY? The painful but honest answer is because I had FAILED HER!

She used to do all the laundry! All the dishes! All the meals! She'd meet me at the door with a smile and a hug. But alas, no more. What an amazing woman that I had been blessed with! All her sacrifices while I was out selfishly pursuing my hobbies. Our life had seemed perfect to me.

While I had been enjoying life, she was asking herself, "Why? Why are these hobbies more important?"

She felt alone and abandoned for years being married to me. Now I live each day feeling her same pain as I continue to wake up alone. How do I help her? How do I help this amazing woman heal? It took me several months, and I know I am not completely there, but I can now see a better path. I can now see who and how I need to be to help her and our relationship heal. With a lot of work dealing with my insecurities, a lot of great coaching, a lot of support and guidance, the path is clear. So many men have given their time to talk with me to get me through the struggles. I know a lot more about what she needs and what my role looks like. I now know how rock-solid I need to be. Going through all this, I am so grateful! I can finally become the man that deep down, I have always wanted to be.

BECOMING
BULLETPROOF

62
INTRODUCTION TO THE DOMAINS

If you have made it this far into the book and you have been integrating the material into your life, here is a snapshot of what you have gathered so far.

You are the masculine bowl in your relationship. Your woman is the feminine water, constantly changing and living in integrity with her feelings. You are the steady, solid, consistent and reliable bowl living in integrity with your terms at all times. You have begun to take 100% responsibility for your life and live with high levels of confidence. You have chosen to trust her 100% and especially to cooperate with her management of the relationship.

By now you have come to know that you are on a hero's journey of growth and you require a tribe of men to journey with. You are proactive in finding a powerful context and never play the victim. You recognize that you are not your bullets and you must remove them from your life. Also you must take ownership for how you behaved because of those bullets.

If you have taken on this work deeply, then you have come to accept yourself as a human man, not as a man hiding behind a mask of perfection, but simply as a masculine human man. You aim to live with high integrity, high accountability, and high trust in your relational bank account.

If this describes you, then you have already become what we call a "one-percent-er,"[20] you are a truly rare masculine man in our day and age.

The following chapters named, "The Domains," are about making your whole life bulletproof at the highest level. Each domain has four levels: Surviving, Self-sufficient, Thriving, and Bulletproof. If a man can make his life bulletproof in all the domains, he will have the safest, most consistent and reliable life possible. Mastering these domains will protect your marriage and family for the years to come.

Make sure as you go through these domains to be gut-level honest with yourself about where you are really at and what it will take for you to get to the next level. Don't lie to yourself, because eventually these domains will give you a slap just like your wife did. For example, if you aren't honest with your physical domain, eventually cancer or a heart attack will slap you and wake you up. Or if you aren't honest about your budget and cashflow, eventually those interest rates will creep up and hammer you. So heed my advice, be honest with yourself. Then push forward!

20| David Goggins recently shared a quote from Heraclitus the Greek Philosopher regarding "one-percenters." "Out of every one hundred men [in battle], ten shouldn't even be there, eighty are just targets, nine are the real fighters, and we are lucky to have them, for they make the battle. Ah, but the one, one is a warrior, and he will bring the others back." Those that live the philosophy of TBH, those are the one-percenters of husbands.

63
INTEGRAL
DOMAIN

"When you are able to maintain your own highest standard of integrity no matter what others may do – you are destined for greatness."

– Napoleon Hill

The integral domain is about how much you are being yourself – the real you – and how much others know the real you. It's about clearing away anything blocking you from being the real you (i.e. bullets). This domain is about having the freedom to be yourself. To have integrity, you will need three components:

1. You will need to know what you want (you will have a goal or direction).
2. You will need to know what you will not compromise (your terms).
3. You will need to be ambitiously pursuing what you want (your purpose).

The strength of the integral domain is equal to the strength of your masculinity. If your integrity is operating at 7/10, then you will feel the strength of your masculinity as a 7/10. As with all the domains, there is a sliding scale that you can rate yourself on.

After basic *surviving*, the first measurement is *self-sufficiency*. Being *self-sufficient* in the integral domain is simply *knowing your terms and purpose and keeping your word*. This may seem like a simple thing, yet most men are not consciously aware of their terms, they are struggling to figure out and pursue their purpose and keeping their word seems like an idea from a bygone era. If a man can step into the requirements of *self-sufficiency* in this domain, it already will give him a major edge in life.

The next step up the scale is to be *thriving* in your integral domain. To be *thriving* is to be reliable with your terms, purpose and the keeping of your word. This is more difficult than it sounds. There is a big difference between *knowing* these three things and being *reliable* regarding these three things. To move up the scale to becoming reliable will require a lot of emotional work to pull the bullets that are getting in your way.

Once you have become reliable, you can press on to the highest level of being *bulletproof* in the integral domain. To be *bulletproof* is to be unshakeable in living your terms. You are consistently true to who you are without any guilt or shame. The pull and expectations of others falls away. And others can accurately describe you because you own your past and have nothing hidden.

Also, once you are operating at this highest level of integrity with yourself and your terms, you become specific about what you participate in and who you partner with. This level of integrity requires that you are careful to align all aspects of your life with who you really are.

DOMAINS HOMEWORK

1. What do I want?
2. What will I ambitiously pursue?

3. Who is in alignment with that purpose?
4. Who is not and will be left behind?
5. What is my integrity structure (relationships and habits) to ensure I own myself and pursue my purpose?

64
EMOTIONAL DOMAIN

"When a man is prey to his own emotions he is not his own master."

— *Baruch Spinoza*

Instinctually, men are hunters, killers and takers. Emotional self-control is expected of men, but there are not a lot of good resources for men to learn self-control. On the other end of the spectrum, women need to feel taken care of and safe. And a major part of her feeling safe comes from knowing that he is responsibly taking care of his emotions.

Being *self-sufficient* in the emotional domain means using exit strategies, containing your anger, being complete with your parents, not blaming others, not seeking approval or being a pleaser, having no one else control your feelings, and knowing that you appreciate your upbringing and wouldn't choose to change anything. It is removing all defensiveness, justifying, arguing, or criticizing, all of which come from bullets. Lastly, it involves you being past the fear of rejection and of looking bad. To move from basic *survival* to *self-sufficiency* in the emotional domain is quite a trek, and to simply arrive at *self-sufficiency* is a major accomplishment. Yet there are two higher levels available.

To move into *thriving* is to move from controlling your emotions to sharing your feelings in an effective and responsible way. When you are at the *thriving* level, you communicate your feelings in a way that others feel safe with. Also, you proactively deal with bullets; you don't suppress your feelings.

Being *bulletproof* in the emotional domain means that you are past emotional reactions. You have become a master at creating the emotions that you want to experience. At this point, you have mastered using context, and your feelings rarely run the show. You sustain your emotional life at the highest level of risk-taking and confidence. You would be described as solid and confident yet also open and vulnerable.

DOMAINS HOMEWORK

1. Where am I still being triggered?
2. What is my integrity structure (relationships and habits) that ensures I am maintaining a high confidence and dealing with triggers?

65
PHYSICAL DOMAIN

Throughout history, men have traditionally been warriors, and part of being a warrior is ignoring pain for the good of the community. This was a necessity for protecting the family, yet nowadays men need to recognize that taking care of their own physical body helps protect their family.

Your body is your access to life on Earth. Improving it improves all domains. Your productivity, earnings, sleep, willpower, sex life, your place in the pecking order, your enjoyment of life, the ability to play with your kids, your lifespan and quality of life – they all improve with physical health.

When you have moved from *surviving* to being *self-sufficient* in the physical domain, the indicator is that taking care of yourself is a part of your schedule and your budget. You are proactively working to prevent physical breakdown. The mindset that you take on is something like: "I am not my car; it is something I take care of and ride around in, and the same is true with my body." You don't simply follow its impulses, but rather you proactively work to maintain it.

When you move from *self-sufficient* to *thriving*, the new mindset is about having the best body available. You begin to pursue this by working out, getting enough sleep and having a careful diet. You look your best, feel your best and perform your best. *Self-sufficiency* was about maintaining, whereas *thriving* is about improving.

When you are in the *thriving* zone, you are upping your game in physical energy and sexual performance. You are likely to step up your physical appearance, be sharply dressed, have good hygiene and organize your space.

At the highest level, being *bulletproof* is a matter of fine-tuning and optimizing. This is the difference between making sure that you run a few days a week versus having a strict running schedule, a strict diet and perhaps competing in long distance running. Also, the sexual domain moves from simply physical to something deeper, which touches the spiritual domain. Typically when *bulletproof* in the physical domain, there is a mastery of a self-discipline such as martial arts or athletics.

DOMAINS HOMEWORK

1. What are my key performance Indicators (KPIs) in the physical domain (my weight, frequency of working out, caloric intake etc.)?
2. How will I personally know if I am self-sufficient, thriving or bulletproof?
3. What is my integrity structure (relationships and habits) to keep moving toward bulletproof and maintain it?

66
RELATIONAL
DOMAIN

*"Men who do not turn to face their own pain are
often prone to inflict it on others."*

Terrence Real

Over the course of your life. you have likely developed many masks that you wear emotionally. Perhaps you are the powerful CEO at work, the playful jester with your children, the loyal golden retriever with your friends, the dashing prince on date night, the Casanova in the bedroom. The problem with masks is that many men lose themselves behind the mask. Not knowing their terms and constantly playing the part of the mask, it is easy to become a series of masks and no longer feel your actual personhood behind the mask. This is especially true if a certain mask brings you loads of praise, adoration and financial or sexual rewards.

You don't necessarily need to rid yourself of all masks, but to move from *survival* to *bulletproof*, you must master a few levels involving masks.

The first step beyond simply surviving in the relational domain is becoming *self-sufficient*, which equates to being aware of the masks you wear around certain people or in certain areas of your life. You may still disguise some feelings but you are aware you are masking. You are choosing to mask and aware of the weakness you have in various masks.

To move into *thriving* is to fine-tune your masks. You are easily able to switch between your masks. You can step back into being an asshole when you need to, such as to protect your wife at a bar, etc. Or you can step into coaching your children with their homework or being your wife's confidant as needed. Thriving means that all your masks have improved and all your relationships are emotionally growing.

Once you reach *bulletproof* in the relational domain, your relationship to masks actually shifts. At this level, your integrity level is so high that you can live proudly with nothing hidden. You can still use a mask when you meet a new person, yet your wider circles know the real you – the man behind the mask. When *bulletproof* in the relational domain, you have developed yourself into someone that can succeed without masks. A *bulletproof* man in the emotional domain is rare indeed and will make an impact in wider circles and typically leave a lasting legacy.

DOMAINS HOMEWORK

1. Am I still wearing masks or am I known as the man under the mask?
2. What relational structures or habits keep me in integrity with living mask-free?

67
MENTAL DOMAIN

"First tell yourself what you will do then do what you have to do."

Epictetus

It has been said that "Doubt kills the warrior." If you think about it, doubt and uncertainty lead to most arguments. When we doubt, we end up hesitating, and this leads to a loss of focus and a sense of not being in the present moment. That loss of presence feels like a loss of masculinity and feels unsafe to your woman.

This is where the mental domain is so important. This domain is where we find our masculine resilience, willpower and fortitude, which keep us going when motivation has failed.

Being *self-sufficient* in the mental domain is tightly related to the integral domain. The higher your integrity, the more present and focused you will be. When you have integrity issues, such as you not keeping your word, or having unfinished tasks and projects, or being inconsistent with meeting her expectations, it is very hard to be mentally present with yourself or for her. To be mentally present, you must begin capturing and clearing up your integrity issues. Take ownership for the things you haven't completed and get to work on them. Also, to be *self-sufficient* mentally also means you must be managing and boosting your confidence proactively.

From another angle, much of mental domain and masculinity is about being clear:

- Clear about your terms
- Clear about what you want
- Clear about your purpose

Having confidence is a must for the mental domain, without confidence, your decisiveness and clarity disappear.

To be *self-sufficient* mentally, you must have a growth mindset and have dealt with your Stupid bullet. How will you know it is gone? When you are no longer trying to prove you are right, or that you are not stupid or naïve, or you can do it alone. Without the Stupid bullet, arguments are just disagreements without the baggage of competition.

You have moved into *thriving* when you have moved past doubt and moved toward mastery in the mental domain. Mastery means you are thinking strategically, you are gathering knowledge, operating in wisdom, having focus and being powerful. In the *thriving* zone, you can use competition to push yourself further faster, without bullets or ego operating. At the *thriving* level, your lifestyle, entertainment choices and career opportunities all begin to expand toward being someone with increased intellect and creativity.

When you have become *bulletproof* in the mental domain, you start moving "off the map" to being an inventor of a new way. You feel that being good or great mentally is no longer good enough. You feel driven to use your mental ability to take on the unsolved and solve it for the good of society. At this point, no challenge is too big, and others see you as a resource. Your abilities are in high demand and you move from being an expert to being a trainer and coach of others.

DOMAINS HOMEWORK

1. What is the unsolved "thing" that I will solve for the good of others?
2. What challenge will I take on?
3. What abilities or knowledge do I have that will be in high demand?
4. What integrity structure (relationships and habits) will I build to keep pushing forward at a high level?

68
FINANCIAL DOMAIN

"You can make excuses and get sympathy or you can make money and earn admiration, the choice is yours."

Manoj Arora

It's pretty straightforward: being successful in finances raises your self-esteem, helps your purpose and helps you keep your terms.

Moving from *survival* to being *self-sufficient* is not about how much you have; it is about your way of being around finances. When you have become self-sufficient, you will:

- Pay your bills reliably and put aside savings
- Have finished pulling out your Weak and Loser bullets
- Be aware of the monthly profit and loss for your household

When you move into *thriving* in the financial domain, you will be a master of listening to her feelings and commitments around finances. You will feel confident in handling risks and making investments. And you will have eliminated emotional spending. When you make a purchase, it is a choice, not a compulsion.

At the *bulletproof* level, you have clear purposeful goals with a structure for reaching success. You are intentionally generous. You are confident, not simply in past accomplishments, but in your ability to restart and rebuild if needed. Last but not least, you are able to pass on an inheritance of wealth and knowledge.

DOMAINS HOMEWORK

1. Am I confidently pursuing a plan to move to the next level in the financial domain?
2. If my spouse died tomorrow, what would financial stability look like?
3. What integrity structure (relationships and habits) will I use to keep me on track?

69
SPIRITUAL
DOMAIN[21]

"Just as a candle cannot burn without fire, man cannot live without a spiritual life."

– Buddha

Our spiritual beliefs are in large part what makes us unique, but they also have the ability to bring us together. So, what does mastery look like in a domain based solely on our beliefs? In large part, it involves being true to those beliefs.

What it means to be *surviving* in the spiritual domain is struggling with the unknown. It has nothing to do with whether you believe in any higher power or not – your beliefs are your own. To move from *surviving* to *self-sufficient*, you move to being able to manage your own optimism and happiness. For many, the path to having peace with what's beyond our capability to know is knowing

21| Having four co-authors for this book, we decided to have Dr. Gary Menezes write the spiritual domain chapter from his perspective, although we may have slightly differing takes on this topic.

that there is order in the chaos. The universe, God, or anything else, beyond and greater than our simple humanity, which does have it handled. It's finding peace within the chaos, and bringing our own happiness and optimism to our lives.

Thriving in the spiritual domain means taking your beliefs outside of being simply beliefs, and putting them into action in your life. You are doing the work to align your habits, rituals and routines with your morals and beliefs. Your spiritual beliefs become consistent with the way you act, the way you speak and the circumstances of your life. Your spiritual beliefs also bring purpose to an otherwise meaningless life. You are the author of and intimately connected to a guiding purpose for what your life is about, and you are in action fulfilling that purpose.

By the time you are *bulletproof* in your spiritual domain, you are no longer working at being spiritual, you simply are your beliefs. Your life represents your beliefs. You go about living your life in your spiritual way, but the quality of life, ease, confidence, clarity and conviction within which you lead it naturally attract others to you. You often share your beliefs, not as a way to justify or explain, but simply as a contribution and in service of your purpose.

DOMAINS HOMEWORK

1. How well do I handle the unknown? What are my fears, doubts and uncertainties about what I don't know or what we don't know, and how can I find peace there?
2. Where am I acting or living inconsistently with what I say I believe? Do my beliefs need to be challenged or my life realigned?
3. How confident am I when my beliefs are challenged? Do I argue, defend or justify, or simply continue my beliefs while letting them have theirs?

Warning from Dr. Jonathan Welton: Having received my doctorate in ministry, and having decades of experience in church work, through The Bulletproof Husband program and the work of bullet pulling, I came to realize that I had been doing something known as "spiritual bypassing." This is when a person doesn't take care of the other domains of their life, but instead they just try to manage them by being more spiritual. So instead of eating right and exercising, they become more spiritual, instead of saving money and investing it, they just have more faith, etc. Instead of doing the painful work of feeling my suppressed hurts and letting out the buried anger, I had just spiritually bypassed it by doing spiritual types of counseling which kept me in my head and didn't push me to "feel to heal" the buried hurt. Although the spiritual domain is important, having a life that is functioning at a high life in all the domains is vital.

70
SEXUAL DOMAIN

"Our modern sexuality would benefit by moving from 'sexual performance' to spiritual pleasure, from 'show-time' to playtime."

– Sureya Leonara

Many men are mastered by sexuality rather than being masters of their sexuality. Just like the other domains, the sexual domain has levels and can be proactively mastered.

When a man is sexually *self-sufficient*, he has cleaned up the past by doing the emotional work and delivering any necessary BPAs, he no longer carries shame or bitterness about his sexual past, he is not controlled by sexual impulses and his terms in this arena are maintained and protected. When you are in self-sufficiency, you recognize that sex is simply a want and not a need.

To move into the *thriving* zone is to have a high level of confidence in yourself. There is no longer any shame about your body image; there is an acceptance of yourself including sexual desires and fantasies. There is no hesitation about pursuing your wife and initiating sex. You are no longer affected by rejection, and you have pulled out the Weak, Victim and Loser bullets. When you are in the *thriving* zone, you have mastered the art of sustaining sex and pleasuring your wife.

Once you are *bulletproof*, you have moved beyond simply mastering sexual techniques and have moved into mastering sexual energy. You are comfortable feeling sexual attraction to any woman in any situation and know that you can transmute that attraction into spiritual/sexual energy that fuels you. You have mastered your physical/spiritual being to the point of being in control of your ejaculations, including non-ejaculatory orgasms using the microcosmic orbit, and you have mastered your PC muscle to serve you. For a man in the *bulletproof* sexual zone, sex is a physical/spiritual gift that you give to your partner, not something you go to get from your partner.

DOMAINS HOMEWORK

1. What am I going to do to progress in the emotional work to remove shame and bullets in the sexual domain?
2. What BPAs do I need to deliver to clean up my sexual past?
3. What resources can I dive into for moving to the next level in the sexual domain?

A FINAL WORD.

We have arrived at the end of our time together and I have thrown a lot at you. My final word to you is this. What you reap is what you sow. If you want your wife to trust you, give trust first. If you want a peaceful relationship, give her safety. If you want to feel solid and masculine, then do the work to live your terms and keep your word.

If you do the work, you will see the results.

APPENDIX WORKSHEETS

HOLD YOURSELF ACCOUNTABLE WORKSHEET

1. What is your goal or target?
2. How would you measure that you have succeeded?
3. By when will you hit this target?
4. What is the consequence if you don't hit the target by then?
5. Which two men will you tell this plan to and ask for them to call you out if you don't follow through?

THE MINI-BULLETPROOF APOLOGY SAMPLE SCRIPT

Thank you. Thank you for waking me up. Thank you for turning my world upside down because you opened my eyes. I see this whole new world of developing myself that I hadn't seen before. Thank you for letting me see what an asshole I have been to you in our marriage/relationship. Thank you for taking the actions you needed to take to bring me to this place of awareness about myself. I could not have done this without you.

You [wanting to separate/divorce, telling me you love me but are not in love with me, cheating on me (personalize this sentence to your situation)] has opened the door to seeing myself in a way I have not seen myself before. Because you opened my eyes, I see there is a whole new realm for developing myself, which I wasn't aware of before. In that realm, I can see that a lot of growth is needed and there is a ton of work for me to do before I can actually give you what you need in this relationship. I can't really tell you what that work is yet. I am in that discovery process but I can see a bunch of stuff already [list one to three behaviors that you can see that you need to start working on: I have been controlling, manipulative, unfaithful, verbally abusive, an addict etc. Let her know that you are beginning to work on these issues and MAKE NO PROMISES HERE; just inform her you are starting to work on these].

I have started on this journey to better myself as a man, husband and father. I will continue this journey of growth because I see that I need to change. I know that this transformation must be done by me irrespective of what decisions you make about our relationship. And I fully trust that you will do what's best for us and our family – whether it is keeping it together or not.

I do need to ask for your help in all of this, though. This journey is a four-month program to really deal with these insecurities to the point where I can promise you that you will be able to look at me and things will be different. I can't do that just yet. I see an aspect of how I can make these changes permanent and I am starting that work. I am going to need your help to make sure I am on track. I need your help to watch me. To see if it's really going on track, I'll talk to you about it and ask you about it along the way. And once I do something that is permanent, I will come back and tell you about it. Thank you once again for waking me up and opening my eyes.

THE SPOT APOLOGY

A SPOT APOLOGY HAS FIVE COMPONENTS:

1. Acknowledge that you did something wrong. No defending, explaining, etc. Just straight up say that she was right.

2. Communicate that you are not clear about why you did what you did. Be honest and simply say, "I reacted," or "I was triggered," "... and I don't know why," etc.

3. Communicate that you will look into the source of where that behavior came from.

4. Communicate that you will come back and let her know when you have dealt with it permanently. By saying this, you are setting yourself up for the time when you will come back and give her a Full Bulletproof Apology regarding this behavior.

5. Thank her for helping you see that behavior in yourself. This step actually builds her up and keeps you from sounding like a defensive victim.

SAMPLE SPOT APOLOGY

[Her name], you are right. That was wrong of me. I am not sure why I did that. I will work on figuring out what the source of this behavior is. Once I figure it out and have permanently dealt with it, I will come back and let you know. Thank you for highlighting this for me.

POSSIBLE BPAS
(A SAMPLE LIST GATHERED FROM TBH MEN)

1. Ruining special occasions
2. Not doing my best to earn more money
3. Drinking too much

4. Publicly embarrassing my wife because she smoked with friends
5. Controlling and manipulating her
6. Having temper tantrums or sulking and crying when I'm denied sex
7. Being over-emotional and over-opinionated
8. Not defending her from my mother's verbal bullying
9. Never picking up my dirty clothes, even when asked
10. Being late and forgetful and flakey
11. Clinging to her in social settings instead of socializing
12. Being cheap and complaining to her every time I bought her something expensive
13. Not buying her anything after giving birth to our son
14. Lying about an affair I had
15. My severe lack of empathy and making everything about my feelings
16. Putting my friends and family ahead of her
17. Chasing her around the house and suffocating her when she screams at me for space and is trying to get away
18. Making a big scene at our son's circumcision ceremony during the most holy part
19. Being a terrible host at my own wedding
20. Not being a team when parenting
21. Making her responsible for my happiness, self-worth and emotions
22. Not making health a priority and sabotaging hers in the process
23. Acting out of control
24. Pressuring to have sex
25. Gaslighting
26. Manipulating around friends or family
27. Emotionally smothering
28. Threatening to leave
29. Yelling; being aggressive, scolding and intimidating

30. Not listening/arguing
31. Gaslighting/intentionally making her feel stupid
32. Having a pessimistic attitude
33. Trying to look good to the public
34. Protecting my ego/never being wrong
35. Avoiding
36. Talking down to her
37. Constantly pressuring her to be sexual
38. Making her feel unsafe by going through her things and invading her privacy
39. Accusing her of having an affair because she's emotionally detached from the marriage
40. Making her feel guilty about spending time with her family because she needed time away from me
41. Making her feel guilty about working too much when she was being the main financial provider for the family
42. Belittling her as not good enough
43. Threatening her with divorce
44. Avoiding communication
45. Feeling need to be a character in life, not authentic
46. Being controlling of her finances and her business
47. Criticism of her choices
48. Being mean/selfish and punishing her and kids
49. Lack of being worthy and pleasing
50. Making her feel stupid
51. Poor listening/misinterpreting her words
52. Controlling of her independence
53. Guilt
54. Not taking action on her requests
55. Procrastinating
56. Being late
57. Snooping, being controlling, stonewalling, not fixing, being unsupportive, making her feel stupid, lack of pursuit, giving to get, keeping score

58. Anger and verbal abuse
59. Not listening
60. Being sarcastic
61. Being defensive
62. Being judgmental
63. Snooping
64. Pornography
65. Pointing fingers
66. Reversing blame
67. Not supporting parenting
68. Putting her down (house duties, kids, sexually)
69. Disrespectful communication
70. Being verbally/emotionally abusive
71. Selfishness
72. Not being a man of my word
73. Being an absent father/husband
74. Pressuring her for intimacy
75. Emotional abandonment
76. Winning arguments (which I could and should have let go), yelling, arguing, not listening, and shutting her down when she asks for something
77. Throwing a fit, yelling and throwing things around when the house wasn't clean
78. Screaming at her, calling her a fucking slut
79. Controlling all the money, making her feel like shit anytime she bought something
80. Physically throwing her and pushing her across the room and punching and breaking our bedroom window
81. Being a victim
82. Lying

COMPLETION WITH PARENTS

As of (today's date):

With my mother I am:

1. Idolizing
2. Rebellious
3. Approval-seeking
4. Accepting
5. Complete (I have no more blame for her and have received the gift of her unconditional love)

With my father I am:

1. Idolizing
2. Rebellious
3. Approval-seeking
4. Accepting
5. Complete (I have no more blame for him and have received his gift of masculinity)

TESTING YOUR TRAUMA

- What did you have for breakfast this morning? *"Scrambled eggs and bacon."*
- What happened when you were six years old? *"My friend's older brother stuck his hand in my pants and squeezed my testicles several times."*
- What did you have for breakfast this morning? *"Scrambled eggs and bacon."*
- What happened when you were six years old? *"My friend's older brother stuck his hand in my pants and squeezed my testicles several times."*

Keep switching back and forth between what your last meal was and stating the facts of your traumatic event until you are able to say the facts without emotion and as simply as something mundane that happened like the scrambled eggs and bacon. If you are feeling emotion come up while you are trying to do this exercise, pause and let the emotion out: cry, scream, wail and do whatever you have to do to let the bullet, blame and pain out. Then go back to the exercise.

When you can look yourself in the eyes in a mirror and say your breakfast and your traumatic story with the same clarity, confidence and tonality, then share your story with a male friend by telling him about the switching exercise and do this exercise with him several times.

When you are free of the blame, shame, emotion, trembling, hesitancy and labeling of your experience, you will be standing on the other side with major freedom from a deep traumatic bullet.

EIGHT DOMAINS AND FOUR LEVELS

As of (today's date) (circle where you are in each domain):

INTEGRAL

Surviving | Self-sufficient | Thriving | Bulletproof

EMOTIONAL

Surviving | Self-sufficient | Thriving | Bulletproof

PHYSICAL

Surviving | Self-sufficient | Thriving | Bulletproof

RELATIONAL

Surviving | Self-sufficient | Thriving | Bulletproof

MENTAL

Surviving | Self-sufficient | Thriving | Bulletproof

FINANCIAL

Surviving | Self-sufficient | Thriving | Bulletproof

SPIRITUAL

Surviving | Self-sufficient | Thriving | Bulletproof

SEXUAL

Surviving | Self-sufficient | Thriving | Bulletproof

What do you need to do to advance to a higher level in each domain?